MIRACLES ON MY MIND! DEVOTIONS TO LAST A LIFETIME...

DELIVERANCE FROM CHURCH HURT AND THE OCCULT...
WALKING IN THE SUPER NATURAL POWER OF GOD

Apostle Dr. Julie Jones

To order additional copies of this book, contact:
Xlibris
844-714-8691
www.Xlibris.com
Orders@Xlibris.com

KJV
Scripture quotations marked KJV are from the Holy Bible,
King James Version (Authorized Version). First published
in 1611. Quoted from the KJV Classic Reference Bible,
Copyright © 1983 by The Zondervan Corporation.

ISBN: Softcover   978-1-6641-2760-9
        EBook   978-1-6641-2759-3

Print information available on the last page

Rev. date: 09/18/2020

This book is dedicated to my parents. Their unending love and support prompted and encouraged me to soar with the wings of an eagle flying far beyond the Alps just before sunset. They provided the gust of wind that compelled my wings to fly to heights unknown. The patience they exemplified, my upbringing in the church, and their selflessness is unsurpassed. For the sacrifices, the sound and Godly advice, and the joys throughout my formative years and beyond, I am eternally grateful. All the prayers made a remarkable difference in my life. Your patience and inspiration of a lifetime enabled me to muster up the courage and strength to submit this manuscript for publication. I arose from the shadows of bashfulness and complacency to share the integral parts of me that God has entrusted me to proclaim. A simple thank you seems so insufficient. From my heart of hearts, I say unreservedly, "Thank you times a million!" I love both of you dearly! The sequel is forthcoming, and my other writings will follow.

I share this special poem I wrote in their honor for their 57th year marriage celebration.

57 Years (My Parent's Marriage Celebration)

The Golden Years....

Today embarks the release of treasured moments untold... Hallmark events commemorate this advent of our finest hour. History now unfolds.

Sacrifice, love, and diligence catapult us to the diamond years.

The threefold cord is deemed inseparable as we defeat all fears.

The bond of family supersedes adversity and human intellect.

We find that, together, we are greater as we gaze in retrospect.

We celebrate before our omnipotent God, ruler and King!

With all of you, we cherish the memories this royal time shall bring.

Most gracious God, we are grateful for the triumphs, joys, blissful times, and even tears.

Hence, we arrived at this momentous occasion of "57" dynamic years for Barbara and Sidney, Mom and Dad, we salute you for the golden years!

You are loved and appreciated beyond measure.

*Now married for 59 years. Glory to God!

My Heart...

God in His infinite wisdom has dealt emphatically with me. He has compelled me to speak a message of inspiration, encouragement, and empowerment to the nations. Amidst the calamities and atrocities of these perilous times, I minister from the heart. I journeyed with the Lord daily until writing became my first love once again. This is a devotional guide designed to provide enlightenment, and it will birth change. I've inserted narratives in my efforts to formally introduce myself. I speak of an astounding deliverance from church hurt and the occult. God led me to proceed on this course before I am allowed to impart more under the anointing of the most high King of Kings. Allow it to speak the essence of you. May it proclaim a message of daily healing to your souls. I embark upon this divinely inspired assignment in prayer that it will minister to the nations of the world. I pray that my words will provide reassurance to last a lifetime. The pandemic of 2020 has brought much disarray. I pause to reflect, to remember, and to honor all those who lost loved ones to Covid 19. All the lives affected by this pandemic, I include you in every prayer. I pray over each and everyone my absolute favorite portion of scripture and rhema word, the prayer of protection, Psalm 91. I hold your courage and efforts in high esteem! I truly believe that God will take us to a place in him where we have never been! We are a people of resilience, versatility, and utmost stamina. We can, and we will arise stronger, greater, and better! We must activate our faith as we pursue our advent into the new! I seek to bring joy, the birth of a more peaceful tomorrow, and newfound strength of a brighter tomorrow. I give you me. I give you my heart. I pray that souls are saved, and I prophesy deliverance, change, and healing.

DEDICATION:

As my sister and friend, I've always admired your drive and determination. I've come to know you as being very intelligent, brave, and a very resourceful person. During our most difficult times, when my husband and I were trying to have a baby, you stood by us during our most trying moments, and I've never forgotten your relentless support with helping us to bring forth our miracle baby. I'm so proud of you and all of your accomplishments, and I'm absolutely certain that your book will inspire and encourage many to accomplish their goals. I'm sure that you will continue to be brilliant and blessed. I love you, and I hope God continues to bless you for many years to come.

Dedication:

"I'm so pleased to see you are accomplishing great things." You are beautiful, highly intelligent, creative, loving, brave, and worthy of your own adoration and affection. Being the third and fourth siblings made me realize how close we were growing up. We had so many great memories together during our childhood and adult life. I named my daughter as your namesake. You're such a great role model to my children, and you comforted me during the time of my bereavement when I lost my fiancé, "Albert Batiste Jr." in May 2018. Heartfelt congratulations on your publication, and I look forward to your future endeavors.

Love always,

Flo, Julie, Marcus, and Ron Jr.

Dedication from my best friend, dearest, Jayda Gros (Andre's/fiancé...beautiful)

Beloved Apostle Dr. Julie Jones, I thank God for sending you to us… You're always ready and willing to share a comforting word and smile. I sincerely appreciate your devotion, your dedication, your love, your spirit, your teachings, and your wisdom. Although you juggle a million things, you're always persistently kind, encouraging, and inspiring to all. I value your presence in my life. I'm proud to call you my friend. You're an exceptional being… my mentor. His greatest blessings for your life is my humble prayer. Warmest congratulations on your first publication. Love you until infinity dearest.

Dedication from Mom and Dad (Mr. & Mrs., Apostle Dr. Sidney Jones, Sr. & Minister Doctor Barbara Ann Jones)

To our beloved, beautiful, and brilliant daughter,

Our hearts are filled with love and gratitude for you. Throughout the years, we realized that you wouldn't be our little girl forever. The Bible says to train up a child in the way he should go; even when he is old he will not depart from it. Through God, we learned how to raise you, and through God you have continued your journey of faith. We didn't have to teach you self esteem, we esteemed God's strength in you.

You are a strong, phenomenal woman who truly loves the Lord. We want you to continue the duties of your ministry and your goals in medicine. Let God's love guide you every step of the way. Be steadfast. Be unmovable. Be yourself. God will lead and guide you.

You are worth more than the world will ever know. We want you to know that we love you. You are also loved by a King, who is bigger than any problem.

Love always, Mom and Dad.

Dedication from Evangelist Cecile Jones Armant (Beautiful sister)

There is no perfect way to write the words to sum up how I feel. You are a beautiful Godly woman, and a gracious dancer. Your faith motivates me. Your faith inspires me. Your faith gives life. There were times when I lost hope, and you reminded me about God's plan. Your passion and your dedication to God's work inspires me to follow God.

I can't begin to tell you how overjoyed I am about your book. I know that it will change lives, create a difference, speak for others, and help the readers to overcome challenges. Your testimony will bless so many.

Sis, you have taught me tons of lessons throughout the years. Ever since I was a little girl, I watched and learned so much from you. I can't wait to see all your future accomplishments in life. I will be right there cheering you on from the sidelines.

Dedication from (Mr. & Mrs.) Bishop Charles Todman & Apostle Dr. Marilyn Todman, CEOs & Founders of Preach the Word Worldwide Network Television (Beautiful, power couple)

Congratulations on writing this phenomenal book. We thank God for your boldness and tenacity. God is truly using you as a guiding light to help women and men become free from past hurts. Your book will bring healing and inspiration to many people around the world.

We are proud to see you blossom in three parts: anointed worship dancer, powerful preacher of the gospel, and now author of this amazing book that will change lives.

Much love and success! May God continue to bless and expand your territory.

Bishop Charles and Apostle Dr. Marilyn Todman.

CEOs and Founders of preach the Word Worldwide Network Television

Acknowledgments:

Many of you saw my potential even in its infancy stages. I give you the accolades for believing that I could achieve all I set out to accomplish. First and foremost, I give God all the glory and adoration, due unto His name. He loved me beyond any realm I could ever deem fathomable. Despite the mistakes, detours, and frailties, He loved me past the pain or any misfortune. He awakened in me the drive to attain success at its highest pinnacle. The eagle mentality, the tiger's eyes, the relentless drive, and quest for the prize have cultivated my intellect. Now, I give you me! My words are sometimes eloquent or simplistic, yet prolific and profound because they were divinely inspired every day of my life through the glorious years.

Special thanks mom for all the prayers and unending support. Thank you for your love and friendship. You never let me give up, and I am eternally grateful for that.

Dad, thank you for standing with me in ministry. You brought much strength, encouragement, and valor. For all the sacrifices, support, and our new building addition at our home, Divine Deliverance Outreach Ministries forever thanks you. Evangelist Cecile Jones Armant my baby sister, I thank you so much for the love, joy, support, and inspiration. You believed in my aspirations and dreams. Now, you are standing with me to see them come into fruition. Your outstanding work of excellence and creative videos of my broadcasts are phenomenally and exquisitely dynamic. To all of my family, my beautiful sisters, Florence and Chaurita I thank you all for the love, encouragement, friendship, and support throughout the years. I appreciate you, and I love you. To my beautiful sister-in-law and future sister-in-law (like sisters), JoAnn and Sandra, I love you two dearly. Thank you for always encouraging. You are a blessing. To my beautiful Goddaughter Cailen, nanny loves you immensely! Keep on attaining your dreams! To all of my beautiful Godchildren, I love you all. You are the children I never had. I thank your parents for sharing you all with me. God bless and protect each of you individually and collectively. To my handsome brothers, Sidney Jr., Reginald, Preston, and Brontell, I love and appreciate all of you. Thanks for offering to beat up any boys who acted up through the years. (smile) I love you all my gorgeous nieces Hannah, Halle, Heidi, Julie (Dr. Dumas), Jalesia, Brianna, Crystal, and princess Ali. To my handsome nephews, Sidney IIII (Brittany/ Dr. Jones), Shane, Marcus, Ron, Reginald Jr., Christopher, Joshua, Jamel, Kameron, Seth, Preston Jr., and Sean, I love you all very much. I love you nanny and Paran (Alcus and Nellie) I love and appreciate both of you. Prayerfully, I hope I didn't forget anyone. Everyone, I love you all dearly. Thank you for your love and support.

Thank you Rev. Dr. Samuel Jones for being a great spiritual father and a dynamic man of God. Through the years, you watched after my soul. I am eternally grateful. All the spiritual leaders who helped me in the grooming process for ministry ~ Rev. Dr. & Mrs. Sidney Tobias, Mr. & Mrs. Samuel Brown, Mrs. Wilhelmena Landry, Mrs. Caldonia S. Ceasar, Mr. & Mrs. Burl Scioneaux, Dr. Jean Farere Dyer, Dr. Fritz Fidele, Attorney Randal Gaines, Mr. & Mrs. (Pastors) Joseph and Joy Jones, Minister of Music, Pastor, and anointed cousin, Ezell Smith Sr., Pastor Prophetess, Rita Sutherland, Pastor Prophet Antoine Graves, Jayda Gros, a forever friend who encouraged me all the time through social media, you rock. To expound upon our bond of strength, I coined the phrase, "dearest." You have been the dearest friend, joy, encouragement, and beautiful sister cheering for me on the sidelines. I couldn't give up. You would never have allowed it. I extend much success to you and Andre, your fiance in your forthcoming marriage. Andre please invite some available, single, Christian, handsome, hardworking, tall, bachelors to the wedding between the ages of 35-45 please, and thank you. All those unspoken, I love and thank you from the heart.

To the CEOs and founders of Preach the Word Worldwide Network Television, I thank you, Mr. and Mrs. (Bishop Charles Todman and Apostle Dr. Marilyn Todman. All you do is in the spirit of excellence.

Bishop, thank you for your patience, hard work, diligence, and commitment to the network and video productions.

Apostle Dr. Marilyn Todman, my birthday twin, (June 3) thank you for being a phenomenal, proverbial 31 woman. I am forever grateful to you for the Godly guidance. You've been a mentor, overseer, a spiritual mother, and all the amazing things, exemplary of a "God fearing" woman. I am so ecstatic that you saw the best in me always. I love both of you dearly. I love and appreciate you Toya, your husband, and the kids. Thanks for looking out for me. I love you like a sister, and you are the epitome of a successful, black woman.

Dedication to You!
(From Apostle Dr. Jones)

It's yours!

Any task you undertake can, in time be done.

Any battle you fight, with God, can be won.

With dedication and perseverance still comes the pain.

With the sunshine's ray of hope, still comes, the rain.

The joy that we'll ascertain brings us much sorrow.

Today brings us pain, but faith holds success for tomorrow.

When most discouraged, we find that we are strong.

Overwhelmed by life's problems, with God we can't go wrong.

Believe in what you are and when you've given all....

Give but a bit more! Arise after a fall.

You control the battle by conquering the daily chores.

When all is done...the prize,

Yes, my friend, it's yours!

Special dedication to a GREAT MAN... A GREAT NAME!

To: George Floyd

WHAT A GREAT NAME…

Your name brought change to kingdoms and nations!

It resonates today and throughout all generations.

Now, we see reformation, restructuring, and no longer shame!

Your cause brings a cry for racial equality, justice, and newfound fame.

The entire world paused to give you honor through your sacrifice.

When we meet again, we'll realize there's more beyond this life!

In life you knew struggles… Rest in heaven! The world will never be the same!

In the end, you've brought new hope! You're a legacy… George Floyd, What a great name!

Live the Dream...

When you want to give a smile, but so often you frown....
When the hardships of this life tend to press you down,
    Live the dream...
When success seems an uncertainty and failure lurks around,
When you wish to speak a word of cheer and cannot utter a sound.
    Live the dream....
When you wish to be a healing presence but your spirits needs mending....
When black America is forsaken, and the struggles are never ending...
    Live the dream
When you cast your cares upon Jesus, and hold on to His hand...
When within your heart you know....
Jesus does understand!"
You have begun, my friend to...
    Live the dream!

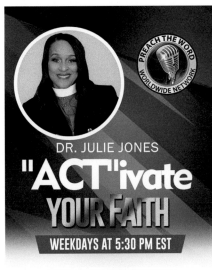

DR. JULIE JONES

"ACT"ivate
YOUR FAITH
WEEKDAYS AT 5:30 PM EST

VISIT WWW.PREACHTHEWORDNETWORKTV.COM
FOR TV DISTRIBUTION

CHAPTER 1

MY GREATEST MIRACLE!

This is one of my, "Let's get acquainted chapters." You'll see more of these in this book. Predominantly, I'm sharing these daily inspirations and poetry with you. They were my "saving grace." As you read the narratives, you'll further understand the spirit of the daily inspirations and motivation. I had to master the art of creating my own sense of solace, peace, and tranquility everyday. The tenacity to thrive is a never ending quest. The next chapter speaks of my greatest deliverance. Prayerfully, you'll continue to read further. I believe you'll be tremendously blessed. The daily devotions kept me grounded. They facilitated my progress. I remained saved. There were some close calls! In the next book, I'll share in depth, my story. Let me begin by saying, I believe in modern medicine. I studied medicine in two foreign countries. I studied for my first two years at a Medical School in Guadalajara, Mexico. I completed the Basic Sciences there. The curriculum included an Introduction to the Practice of Medicine, Community Medicine, and Clinical Skills, and General Surgery Procedures. While we were initially told that the first two years would be taught in English, many lectures were taught in Spanish. When we examined patients in the clinical classes, we had to speak Spanish exclusively. I had to utilize what Spanish I had learned in Undergraduate studies. I immediately started a self study of Spanish in order to matriculate through the clinical courses. Part of my time there, I lived with two different Spanish speaking families which helped immensely. Clinical rotations would be completely in Spanish, so I transferred to an English speaking Medical school in the West Indies thereafter. I spent the required thirty days on the island for ten day intervals. It was required that I passed two review blocks which I did successfully. This afforded me the opportunity to complete all my clinical rotations in my home state of Louisiana in the city of New Orleans. At this time, I can safely say that more Medicine and Research is coming in my immediate future. I didn't start a residency, but I did finish clinical studies in good standing. I finished all my clinical rotations with honors. Thanks be unto God! I also passed my Exit Exam in the West Indies, which was a prerequisite before continuing in the program. I am an advocate of the holistic approach to health and healing. I earnestly believe that spirit, body, and soul must coincide in order to promote true health and healing.

There were pivotal points in my life when writing became my therapy. I reached times of epiphanies and catharses, and these moments enabled me to internalize my spiritual healing and growth. I read the word of God daily and consistently, but the words became life with each encounter, each miracle, and each experience. Shortly after studying clinical medicine, a personal diagnosis would come that would change my life forever. I had begun to apply for residency. I was a senior medical student completing clinical rotations. Hurricane Katrina came, and ravaged most of the southern region. I had gone home to St. James, Louisiana to weather the storm. All was well until I decided to return to Algiers where my home was. Prior to the hurricane, I had previously purchased my first home. It was a two story, French colonial style home. I worked in Medical Research at a hospital on the East bank, and I lived in Algiers. I also worked part time at a medical clinic. (The building was completely destroyed by the hurricane.) The Monday following hurricane Katrina, I made a valiant attempt to check on my home. This turned into a week helping out at a hospital on the West Bank. I won't elaborate further here, but it was mind boggling! I will share more in the sequel. I can say that I travelled about a month before returning to New Orleans. I began to have extreme headaches with the aura. I attributed this initially to the stressful effects of the hurricane. My vision became blurred. I experienced syncope episodes, nausea, and lightheadedness. I noticed physical changes, and even began producing breast milk. I knew there was not a possibility that I was pregnant. I went to the ER at the hospital where I worked. I had to follow up with my own physician afterwards. With these signs and symptoms, I self diagnosed. This is why I gave you the preamble to my story at the beginning of the chapter. My medical background afforded me the knowledge to make the diagnosis of a prolactinoma. As previously noted, the complete story is coming in the next book. I have charts, figures, and graphs. I instructed my physician to order an MRI of the brain with and without contrast. Low and behold, I definitely had a prolactinoma. At this point, I must tell you about the greatest miracle I ever received. My treatment journey began. Oral treatment was initiated, and I became a regular patient to several specialists. The obstetrician/gynecologist made the initial diagnosis. The predominant signs and symptoms led me to this direction first and foremost. Soon afterwards, I was directed to the endocrinologist, a neurologist, an ophthalmologist, and a neurosurgeon. Let me suffice it to say that all these specialists took great care and concern. They all knew about my background in the field of Medicine, so it was awesome that I was well informed. It enabled us to "talk shop!" I understood the medical lingo and jargons. I had the typical signs and symptoms of a prolactinoma. It is a tumor of the pituitary gland in the brain. With prolactinomas, the hormone producing pituitary gland produces too much prolactin. The tumor causing over production of prolactin is benign. It can cause headaches, breast discharge of milk or a milk like substance, irregular periods, infertility, impaired vision, low bone density, and other health problems. Women experience symptoms before men who have the same diagnosis. Men can experience breast enlargement, hormonal disturbances, vision impairment, and erectile dysfunction. (1998-2020 Mayo Foundation For Medical Education) It is still unknown what may cause this type of tumor. In my case, bromocriptine was prescribed initially. The side effects were overwhelming. The headaches on this regimen were so severe that I had to pull aside when I was driving until the headaches would subside. I was also put on an additional medicine to treat the headaches. I gained a considerable amount of weight on the bromocriptine. Then, I was put on cabergoline, which had just as many side effects. In some cases, surgery is inevitable. The endocrinologist started me on the bromocriptine. I followed this regimen for about two years sporadically. The headaches became nearly unbearable. I gained about 50 pounds within four months. My abdomen and breast grew larger which was also a sign of this disorder. Elevated prolactin also caused weight gain. I also had diagnoses of insulin resistance, polycystic ovarian syndrome, and ovarian dysfunction which could all show an increase in weight. For someone who was always into health and fitness, this was quite challenging and disheartening. During this time, I had at least two more MRIs. The last MRI showed dimensions of a tumor that required a visit to the neurosurgeon. It was decided that I would be put on a different medication as I shared earlier, cabergoline. It was one of the newest regimens at the time which would work more aggressively than the first. The side effects, however, were quite troublesome. It was a journey of trial and error. At times, dosages were decreased to lessen the effects exhibited by the drug. After much consideration, many visits to the specialists, vision exams, more signs and symptoms, I was directed to a neurosurgeon. This puts us closer to a discussion of the "super natural!"

The neurosurgeon was excellent, professional, personable, kind, and he had a healing presence. Did I mention that he was extremely handsome? Well, he was extremely handsome. I do have a sense of humor from time to time. He was extremely attentive, and this was so comforting. He understood all the range of emotions I was experiencing. He genuinely cared. His guidance through the medical recommendation was superb. Even though I was carrying fifty extra pounds, he had the ability to lighten the load, so to speak. He explained that all the documentation from the other specialists confirmed that I needed to undergo a surgical procedure to remove the tumor. He explained what the procedure would entail. He added that the results of the visual exam concluded the prognosis. I had several series of visits to the ophthalmologist. All reports confirmed that I had begun to lose peripheral vision in both eyes. Hence, surgery was scheduled. This was a wake up call for me. I had previously had five surgeries to remove fibroid tumors from the uterus. I also had my tonsils and adenoids removed while I was a sophomore in Undergraduate school. I had prayed, and I made it through all the surgical procedures. However, I did not want to have a brain surgery ever. I explained to the neurosurgeon that I was a Christian. I told him that I did not want to have the surgery, but I would comply. I did tell him before I left his office that I would pray not to require the surgery. He smiled, and he looked at me and replied, "I completely understand."

I never prayed as fervently as I did after leaving that office that day. I had to master self encouragement. This is the way I've always been even from a child. I went to all the appointments on my own. The nurses asked me why I was always by myself. They said they cried for me at times, because they saw my courage. I knew mom would worry, so I told her she didn't have to accompany me. Hence, I would go alone. Mom always asked if I needed her to go with me. She had already made it through a brain surgery herself. Her doctor called her the miracle girl! Mom was discharged from the hospital the next morning. Her doctor said he had never released a patient so early following that procedure. He said she was doing so well though. She had to have her skull opened, and she had 22 stitches when she had her operation. I truly believe she went through it all, so I wouldn't have to. She had told me she hoped I would never have to have the brain surgery once we knew my diagnosis. It was a different type of tumor that I had however.

What I didn't realize was that this was the birthing of the "encourager", the "inspirer", and the "empowerer" in me. It would actually be a gift. It would qualify me to walk in the office of an apostle in the years to come. I have to be succinct at this point. I'll condense the story for now. I made a concerted effort to believe God for a miracle. My prayer focus was that I wouldn't have to have the surgery at all. I attended a revival, and I went up to be prayed for. The presiding Apostle asked me what I needed from God. I told him I needed a miracle so I wouldn't have an upcoming brain surgery. He said I had been so faithful to God, and I wouldn't have to have brain surgery. He asked me if I believed that God would heal me. I said yes, I believed. He wanted to know if I'd be checked again by the doctor before surgery. I explained that I was already scheduled for surgery within a matter of days. I told him I did have another vision test scheduled within two days. This was the third vision test I'd have before surgery. The team of ophthalmologist, residents, and medical students told me that the vision exams I had even two weeks prior showed different results. The word they used was "baffled." They said all my peripheral vision was back within normal limits in both eyes. The other vision exams showed loss of peripheral vision in both eyes even two weeks before. This had led to the scheduling of the surgery. The ophthalmologist said he would call the neurosurgeon the same day to notify him of the new findings in my vision. By the time I arrived at home, the neurosurgeon was calling me on my cell phone. He said, "Young lady you are making a believer out of me. If I didn't know you had a brain tumor, I would have though you never had one. I can't operate on a shadow. You received your miracle. Your surgery was cancelled." This was, and still is the greatest miracle I ever received! Once an encounter like this occurs, everything else just seems so trivial. You realize what a powerful God we serve. A praise and a worship erupts inside you that causes the fire of God to burn anything that is not like Him! Criticism, ostracism, humiliation, or discrediting have no effect. Six days prior to surgery, the procedure was cancelled. My peripheral vision was restored fully in both eyes. The smile never left after this day. It was a hallmark event that would forever change my life. Writing, reading the word, and praying were my strength and my joy. Later, I would lose the fifty pounds plus more which comes in the next book. While we're just in the "getting acquainted" stage, I won't divulge "all" at this time. I've inserted many inspirational writings to comfort, bring tranquility, and to prepare you for a mindset for miracles. This was my first encounter with the prolactinoma.

Approximately three years later, I was faced with the same signs and symptoms that the prolactinoma initially brought. After an MRI, it was confirmed that the tumor was beginning to rear its head again. This time, God curtailed it expediently. The cabergoline treatment was recommended once again. The side effects were eventually intolerable. I prayed incessantly. I saw a neurosurgeon. (A different one… The other neurosurgeon had relocated.) He decided I should try to tolerate the medication. Surgery would still be an option if the growth of the tumor didn't subside. I distinctively remember seeing another neurosurgeon I knew when I was completing clinical rotations in medical school. This neurosurgeon told me we would believe that I'd never have to face surgery for this disorder. He said the size of the tumor was right between surgery and no surgery. He said vision changes would also be a deciding factor. The vision tests later revealed all fields were within normal limits in both eyes. It was at this point when I made a conscientious effort to pray, get the yearly MRIs as directed, see the endocrinologist, and never expect surgery. Eventually, the neurologist said I could discontinue any visits. He said these tumors have a way of exhausting themselves. Even without taking the medications regularly, I began to feel so much better. Surgery has never been discussed again. God is still working miracles. It is my earnest prayer that someone's faith is increasing!

CHAPTER 2

OVERCOMING THE SPIRIT OF INFIRMITY

I want to share about the encounter I had of a severe asthma attack at the age of six. The doctor said I was very sick at the time. I had been playing at home, and all of a sudden, I could hardly breath. I went to my mom and told her that I couldn't catch my breath. My breathing became so labored that my mom took me in her arms, and she told dad I would have to be rushed to the hospital. On the way there, my parents put all the windows down to facilitate my breathing. By then, I was gasping for air. Even at six years old, I knew I was very ill. The doctors said we arrived at the hospital just in time. I was put on oxygen, and the doctors said I'd have to have a tracheostomy. A surgical opening would be done at the front of the neck, and a tubing would be placed there to provide an opening for breathing. Everything was happening so quickly, but I remember the doctors telling my mom things didn't look good. I recall my mother holding me closely, and she prayed the Our Father prayer. I also heard her say, "Lord heal my child. Lord heal my child." Within minutes, the doctor returned. The outcome was that the tracheostomy didn't have to be performed, and the doctors said they didn't know what happened. I went from needing the surgical procedure to being discharged within a span of a couple of hours is how I remember it. My mom was concerned about possible future attacks, and the doctors felt something like a miracle happened. We were told that no one as sick as I was upon arrival just walks right out not long after. It just didn't happen that way. Mom knew it was a miracle that happened that day. This was my first miracle that I have a recollection of.

I never had an asthma attack again. I remember when I was about 10 years old, I had a severe bout of croup, also known as laryngotracheobronchitis. The condition causes swelling inside the trachea, and normal breathing is interfered with. I had a straining cough, fever, and hoarseness. (Wikipedia, McMillian, Retrieved 1 April 2020) My cough sounded like a barking noise. I had all the typical signs and symptoms of the disorder. It hurt to cough and breath. It was different from the time I had the asthma attack however. My grandmother told mom and dad to take me to the doctor, because the cough sounded so peculiar. Once I was taken to the doctor, I was diagnosed with croup. My symptoms were treated, and I returned home. I was sick for at least a week. I was such a happy little girl that it was difficult to decipher when I was not feeling well. I smiled all the time. People always commented on my smile. They said it was beautiful. They said it was a gift to the world. I always received compliments that I was beautiful, blessed, brainy, and born again. My optimism was birthed so early in my childhood. I always encouraged any and everyone I knew. I smiled even when I was the sickest I could ever be. I always had dreams and aspirations of being in ministry and medicine. I would forever say that I wanted to dedicate my life to Christ and to helping others. Any opportunity I had, I helped others. Mom said I was so smart and inquisitive at the same time. I would read, write, study people, and work on "projects" much of the time. I was very close to my grandparents on my father's side of the family. My dad's mother told me that July of 1980 would be her calling year. I was very close to her and dad's father. We lived in the Jones' yard. I walked to their house everyday. I would make them coffee and cheese toast. Grandma said I made the best coffee ever. I said, "Don't worry grandma, I will make it for you everyday!" She would also have me to wash her rice whenever I was there. They were so wise, and grandma told me her dreams all the time. Grandma left us in July of 1980 as she prophesied. My grandfather died a few days later. I'll never forget the blue and pink caskets in the church. I was devastated!! I was thirteen years old, and my closest and best friends had left me. I cried to no end!!! There were so many of us grieving their loss. My mom's mother died before I knew her. I remember my mother's father. He lived in our home briefly. I mainly remember I was three years old when mom's dad, Felix Whittington died. I still have the little, navy suspender dress I wore with a white shirt. Mom kept it all these years. She preserved a great deal of our garments and momentos. Mom was a seamstress, and she baked delicious homemade pies that were sold at chemical plants. Mom sewed wedding gowns, bridesmaid dresses, suits, and all types of clothes. We would wear such nifty outfits that people would look for the tags inside our garments. It was difficult to believe that mom would sew such beautiful clothes. Mom was extremely gifted. She finished at the top of her high school class. She said she was selected to recite 6 page narratives. She entered speech competitions, and she would do very well. Mom tried out to be a majorette in high school, and she was selected. She later decided she was too shy. She told me that she won a scholarship to study nursing. Instead, she made a decision to marry my dad, and she gave birth to seven beautiful children. She had three boys and four girls. She said if she had to live her life all over again, she wouldn't change a thing. She taught me so much, and she imparted a great deal of wisdom. Mom was formally ordained as a minister, and she received a doctorate in Divinity from universal L.C.M. in September 2020. Dad was an excellent and gifted carpenter. He could build anything! He built houses from the ground up. He built our first home, and he built the second one as well. The current house was renovated, and it has six bedrooms. It is an anointed and grand home. Dad is an ordained minister of the gospel. On Mar 22, 2019, dad was affirmed as an Apostle, and he received a doctorate of Divinity from American F.C. Dad taught us many principles, and he also imparted much wisdom. He always talked to us about budgeting money. When we had just moved into the new home, he paid out for the house within three years. The house is grand, and it has been appraised for $350,00.00 value. All glory to God. Dad recently built a new addition to our home, which is the new site of Divine Deliverance International Outreach Ministries' Headquarters and recording studio. I have a professional video choreographer who comes on site to record my television shows. The shows are submitted to Preach the Word Worldwide Network Television. I have my own show on this television network, "Activate your Faith!" It airs every Monday through Friday at 4:30 pm central time. I am eternally grateful, and I am ecstatic about this opportunity. By divine appointment, God connected me with Apostle Dr. Marilyn Todman and her husband, Bishop Todman, CEOs and Founders of the Television Network. Initially, I became a TV promoter for the Network. I was already featuring a broadcast on the Now Television Network. I had my own show entitled, "Mindset for Miracles!" I do not currently have the show on the Now Network. Preach the Word offered me my own show, which I excitingly accepted!! I traveled to Atlanta every six weeks to have four shows recorded. I absolutely loved the experience. Due to the Covid 19 Pandemic, I am still having the shows filmed at my studio here in Louisiana. As of today, I am still preaching on Worldwide television.

When I was in the sixth grade, I was playing barefoot in an open field. I was running, and I stepped on a broken glass. I was bleeding quite a bit, and I couldn't walk any further. My cousin ran to get my mother. Mom saw that the cut looked rather deep. I had to be rushed to the ER. I had to get seven external stitches and two internal stitches. I was given crutches, and mom and my aunt were about to take me home. As I used the crutches, the wound started bleeding again. It bled all down the hallways. The incision had to be worked on again. I had cut an artery. The glass had gone all the way through to the top of my foot. I could have nearly bled to death is what the doctor said. I was pretty shaken up, but I was happy to be alright. I had to miss a few weeks of school and have my lessons sent to our home. I'm just giving a synopsis of events that shaped my belief of miracles throughout my encounters. In the midst of it all, I still had an awesome childhood. I took piano lessons during my sixth grade year. My teachers wanted to have me skipped a grade, because they felt I wasn't challenged enough. Mom decided I should remain with my peers. I preferred to. I loved to play with Barbie dolls. I loved writing poetry and reading. I was extremely shy when it came to stage performances. I would write poetry, and the principal would commend me. He would request that I read my poetry at assemblies. Through crocodile tears, I would manage to recite the poetry at school events. I wrote essays, short stories, and the poetry. I would win money, trophies, and awards. Eventually, I began to outgrow the stage fright. I would write plays, and I'd star in them. I went from extreme stage fight to playing the leading roles. I would compete in state speech competitions. I would place in the top ten of sixty-four parishes. I couldn't just share the illnesses without sharing some of the phenomenal memories and victories. Mom said I was/am very intelligent. I made straight As. I was given the valedictorian address by my teachers to recite at my sixth grade graduation. I was the top student in my class in elementary school. I was among the top students in my junior high and high school classes. I was voted the most popular girl by my peers in Junior High and High school. I won the award for the top English student in my graduating class by Ms. Griffin. She was extraordinary, and she was very tough. I felt so honored to receive that award. Ms. Griffin had told me that on class night I would find out what type of English student I was. I was the captain of the cheerleaders in Junior High, and I was a cheerleader for the St. James Wildcats throughout high school. My peers looked up to me, and they said I was a light unto them in many ways. I adored and encouraged them all. They motivated me to be a leader even the more. I ran track in high school as a senior. The track team was just starting up for the girls when I was a senior. I led warm up exercises, and I encouraged the team to just do their best. Their efforts were rewarded. We had a very strong and successful track team. I ran the 440 relay, the 880 relay, and the 400 (open quarter). I won first place in district in the 400. (District champion 1985) I was so ecstatic, because I beat the LHS top runner in the 400. (No one did that!!!) I qualified for state as well. All glory to God!! I have lots of medals, ribbons, and trophies from track, writing, modeling, 4-H speech competitions, science fairs, and social studies fairs, general competitions, and safety poster contests, library club contests, Catholic daughters poetry contests, etc. In High school, I was informed by the principal that I was the top black student in my high school graduating class. I graduated with high honors, and I had an "A" average. Mom said I excelled in the sciences especially, and she said I would complete my own science and social studies projects. I would win, and I'd go to the regional fairs as well. I'm sharing this to say that there was a great deal of joy also. The good days far superseded the setbacks.

As we continue to get acquainted, I remember my first surgery was when I was a sophomore (1987) in Undergraduate school. I had my tonsils and adenoids removed. As early as elementary school, I'd have severe bouts of tonsillitis. During these intervals, I wouldn't be able to eat for several days or swallow. I would sometimes lose a substantial amount of weight. My parents took great care of me always. They would take me to our family physician. I'd be prescribed antibiotics, low dose pain meds, and sometimes I'd get injections. Sometimes, I had to stay home from school. The tonsillitis would persist for days at a time. By the time I entered college, the bouts would be so frequent that my doctor suggested that I had my tonsils removed. Even after the obstacles, I entered Dillard University as a University Scholar. It was the highest honor bestowed upon any entering freshman. I was a Presidential Scholar in which I had a full tuition paid scholarship for four years. I studied pre-medicine Biology with a minor in English. I was an Ella A. Tackwood Scholar, an Emily B. Morrell Scholar, A Howard Hughes Scholarship recipient, an MBRS scholar, a member of the Biological Honor Society (TRI BETA), Natural Sciences Honor Society (BETA KAPPA CHI), Comparative Vertebrate Morphogenesis Tutor, Botany tutor, Calculus tutor, Reading and Writing lab tutor, High School Writing tutor at John McDonough High School, Essay Award winner for Black History/Junior Year, Top Ten on English Proficiency Exam all years taken, Study Abroad Scholarship Recipient, Studied in Angers, France for one Summer & visited Paris, France, Special Assignment Intern For the Black College Fund, Board of Higher Education and Ministries, United Methodist Student Movement President, Junior Year, Runner up as Junior attendant to Miss Dillard, Contestant for Miss Dillard Senior year (Placed in the top four), Health and Fitness Videos, Volunteer at Ochsner Clinic Foundation/Assistant to the Child Psychologist… Panelist for Pre-Medicine Forum/Senior Year. I would enroll in 21 semester hours each term, and all the courses were honors level. I completed all my graduation requirements a year early. As the saying goes, "I wasn't chopped liver!" The Bible says, "O give thanks unto the Lord; call upon his name: make known his deeds among the people. Sing unto him, sing psalms unto him: talk ye of his wondrous works." Psalm 105:1,2 We have official bragging rights. The Bible also says, "And they overcame him by the blood of the Lamb, and by the word of their testimony; and they loved not their lives unto death." Revelation 12:11 Many scriptures are covered in part two of this book, but I had to pause here to include these.

My second surgery was in 1989. I was a senior, undergraduate student. I had to have uterine fibroids removed. It was performed at a hospital in New Orleans east. The surgery was successful. I graduated from Dillard University the same year with above a 3.2 grade point average. I went to Nashville, Tennessee where I pursued Biomedical Sciences Research at a Medical College there. I was also accepted to pursue graduate studies there in the Departments of Physiology and Pharmacology. At that time, I opted to pursue Physiology. I prepared for the MCAT (Medical College Admissions Exam) At the end of my first year in research, I met a gentleman who was a senior in the medical school. We began dating, and eventually I moved to Buffalo, New York where he started residency in Physiatry (Physical Medicine and Rehabilitation.) I studied for the exam, enrolled in Post Baccalaureate studies at SUNY Buffalo, worked two jobs, and I modeled bikinis for Syndicate Productions. I was always very innovative. I was driven by my ambitions. My relationship was an interracial relationship. He encouraged me to continue my pursuit of medical school. I took the MCAT in Buffalo, New York. I did well. I applied to a few schools the year I was in Buffalo. I interviewed at two medical schools out of the five I applied to. One interview was where I did Biomedical Sciences research, and the other interview was in my home state of Louisiana. (LSU/ New Orleans) I was on the waiting list at both Schools. I made a decision to move back to Louisiana, and I applied to foreign medical schools. I received multiple acceptances to Medical schools Abroad. Hence, I accepted my offer to study medicine in Guadalajara, Mexico. More of the story comes later. This is our time of getting acquainted.

Within about three years, I was faced with another surgery to have fibroid tumors removed. I was also diagnosed with endometriosis. The surgery was successful. However, I would go on to face three more surgeries through the years for removal of uterine fibroids. I was also diagnosed with insulin resistance, polycystic ovarian syndrome, and ovarian dysfunction. I frequently went to medical appointments from time to time to have the conditions monitored. I was not trying to start a family, so I was not aggressive about measures to combat infertility issues. Despite all, I remained cheerful. I always smiled, and I was always optimistic. It was ingrained into my DNA.

Fibrocystic breast disease was another diagnosis. I was told by my doctor to avoid caffeine as much as possible. My condition was monitored very well. I began having mammograms by the age of 45. Our family history was prevalent for breast cancer and other types of cancer. From 2015 to 2019, I had to have repeat mammograms because of a suspicious mass seen in the left breast. First, I had the mammogram. I was called in for an ultrasound. Then, I had to have a repeated mammogram. Each year, I received letters that stated I had no evidence of cancer! My last surgery to remove fibroids was in 1993. Since then, I never had to have another procedure for the condition. I consider this a major victory over that spirit of infirmity!!! God is so AMAZING!

CHAPTER 3

Meeting Mr. Tall, Dark, And Handsome

I had just been on a forty day and forty night fast. (It started in January 2006.) God was ministering to me in so many areas. I was back in a size five, and I was at my healthiest. The pictures that precede this section are from the photo shoot I had for my fitness project and first DVD. I was 39 years old, and people thought I was in my 20s. I would get asked out by guys in their 20s all the time. In other words, when the "leader" met me, I had it going on. (smiles) I took care of myself in every way. I bathed in special oils. I went to the dentist regularly. I had regular checkups at the doctor. I still worked in the medical field. I was a very hard worker. I brushed my teeth throughout the day, and I flossed at least twice a day. I dressed well. I had my hair done regularly, and I spent whatever it cost. I wore obsession cologne which I received many compliments always. I wore "Victoria's Secrets" lotions, fragrances, etc. I was said to be the complete package. Still, I do all these things. I was also confident, and I had a lot of other guys who were interested in me. I received many compliments all the time. The "leader" later said that I was the size five woman God had shown him who would be his wife. In order to present the full story, I had to include these details. I was leading others to their weight loss goals, so I had to maintain spirit, body, and soul. If I just told you what I looked like, someone could have put a disclaimer on it. The pictures help me to tell the story. By the time, I left the organization, I was back to what I looked like when I arrived at the church for the first time. However, it didn't matter what I looked like to "them". I was eventually ridiculed no matter how much I gave, how I looked, or how much God had put inside me. Nothing at all mattered to the "leader."

I prayed for many who received healings, financial blessings, breakthroughs, etc. God showed me prophetic dreams. Individuals confirmed the validity of the dreams. One in particular was that I had seen mom was involved in a car accident. The car was struck from the rear. When I called mom, she said she had been involved in a car accident, and the car was struck for the rear. She was doing well. She said she didn't want me to worry about her. I was still living at my home in Algiers. I had also dreamt that mom was bit on her leg, and she had a severe reaction from the bite. When I called her, she confirmed having been bitten by an insect. She had a severe reaction to the bite. There were other dreams. In June of 2005,

God showed me a dream. He said to me clearly and alarmingly, "It is "ark building" time!" I remember the dream coming before me again as I was standing in my garage at my home in Algiers. I immediately called mom on the phone to tell her what God told me. Mom said pray, because that is a premonition. You have to pray!! I prayed, and I had begun a fitness and health project for the body of Christ. I went to different churches to give seminars regarding fitness and health. I utilized my knowledge from medical school, and I was a certified personal trainer with NESTA, a certified aerobics instructor via Expert Rating, a Wellness & nutrition instructor, hip hop and kick boxing classes instructor, and step aerobics instructor with the French Riviera. I told as many Pastors as I could what the Lord had told me. "It's ark building time!" My fitness group and I went to Congo Square in New Orleans during the Essence Festival, and we did an aerobics DVD. I gave talks about fitness and health, and I marketed my first fitness DVD and originally written songs that I wrote for the project. The project was, "Living Sacrifice for the body of Christ!"

It was based on Romans 12:1,2

1. "I beseech you therefore, brethren, by the mercies of God, that ye present your bodies a living sacrifice, holy, acceptable unto God, which is your reasonable service.

2. And be not conformed to this world: but be ye transformed by the renewing of your mind, that ye may prove what is that good, and acceptable, and perfect will of God."

We had a successful event, and we reached a great deal of people. God blessed me to make the money I had invested in the project and more. Jehovah Jireh kept on providing. By August 2005, God confirmed my dream. Hurricane Katrina would come, and waters would cover much of the southeastern region. It was the beginning of many sorrows. Over three thousand people were known to have lost their lives. Even though I wasn't as deeply into the things of God as I had desired to be, God still spoke to me often. I would always share with my mother what God had shown me or told me. She was always able to be a witness to the truths that I shared with her. The conditions became deplorable in some areas, and we faced many calamities. I felt prepared in the sense that God had given me a premonition. My discernment was beginning to increase in leaps and bounds. I was so grateful to God. Now, maybe you will understand why I believed so fervently that the leader I met was to be my husband. God continuously showed me things, and he confirmed so much in my spirit. The 40 day fast I was on ended on Valentine's Day 2006. I would never forget it. I had seen God do so much for so many individuals during that time. Consequently, I asked God to do the "hard" thing. I asked him to allow me to meet my husband that day, February 14, 2006. Once I had dressed for the day, I called mom to ask her if she wanted to go to BR to get our hair done. She said yes. We had a regular hair appointment schedule with this beautician, so we'd be going on an unscheduled day. The beautician agreed to give us appointments. I made several stops along the way. I had previously written a list to God as to what criteria my husband should exhibit. When we arrived at the shop, I saw a man having his hair washed. Time evolved, and by then I was under the hair dryer, and mom was under a hair dryer also. I looked up, and the man who was having his hair washed upon our arrival was standing up 6' 3", tall, dark, and handsome looking like a dream come true. He was my "list!" I was 5'6". I wore a size five, and I had just trained for a professional fitness DVD. I have included photos as proof. He later told me that I fit the description of his future wife. I whispered a comment to mom about the man. I asked one of the stylist who the man was, and she said, "Oh, that's J's ex." I reclined, and I continued reading a book. Afterwards, J approached me. I asked her if the man standing a distance away was her ex. She replied, "No!" She said he's my Pastor. He's the man I've been telling you about. I have wanted the two of you to meet. I think you two would really hit it off. J walked over to the man who proceeded to walk towards the dryer that I was under. He said hello as I did also. Then, he said he would get his card from his vehicle. He returned with it, and he gave it to me with his cell phone number written on the back. He said, give me a call, and we can get together. I gave him one of my cards as well. I wrote my cell number on the back. I told him that I'd talk to him soon. Within a couple of days, we had arranged to go to dinner. We went on a dinner date in his home city. We had an amazing time, and we decided we would go out again. We talked and shared. He said what he loved most was I was subdued about his title in ministry, etc. I was more concerned about getting to know the man. He said you know I'm an Apostle and a Pastor. I said that is excellent, and I just smiled. I knew I wanted to know more. By April 2006, I was a member of his church. This was an introduction of what led to the remainder of the story. I'm making a valiant effort to explain the story without giving all the details now. I'm giving you the relevant events leading to the major happenings. The first time I attended his church, mom was with me. It was a morning service. His sermon was so impressive and filled with the fire of God that I wanted to attend the evening service. Dad met mom and I, so mom could go home. I attended the evening service. This man preached with an anointing much like Bishop T. D. Jakes. No one impressed me more than the honorable Bishop. This leader did impress me in the same manner!! He had the voice of roaring thunder, and his fire struck like lightening bolts!!!!! I was surely attracted to his anointing first and foremost. This is what made me stay for so long after the inevitable end of our relationship. He indeed preached the horns off a "Billy goat!" (As the saying goes...)

CHAPTER 4

DELIVERANCE FROM CHURCH HURT

My encounter with church hurt was an integral part in the cultivating of my calling to the office of an apostle. I will make no mention of specific names or churches. My goal here is to be instrumental in the deliverance of others, especially women who experienced similar struggles and obstacles as I did in ministry. I call you out of the shadows of shame, misunderstanding, and misconceptions to divine deliverance, freedom, and liberty! Arise, and take your rightful place in the kingdom queens and kings! Someone is counting on you to assist in their deliverance. I decree, and I declare that you shall come forth, and be all God destined you to be. I speak to every broken place, every catastrophic memory, every residue of abuse, every hurting place, every heartache or heartbreak, every tear, every pain, every moment of discontentment… I speak healing, deliverance, and restoration this day in the name of Jesus!

I must rewind in order to quickly advance you to the present. I joined the ministry in question in April of 2006. (Post hurricane Katrina and Rita) I reiterate, I had previously met the leader of the organization before I attended service. We were introduced by a mutual friend. The mutual friend was told by the leader that he had taken me on a date. I received a call from the mutual friend who told me she was aware that I had gone on a date with the leader. I confirmed that this information was valid. As time progressed, I decided to attend service at the ministry. The leader and I remained friends, and within a few months, we started dating secretly. He said the relationship had to remain private, because the church people had to be prepared when he would announce that we were a couple. I accepted his request to keep the "entanglement" a secret, if you will. He specifically told me that he would marry me once we were positioned spiritually. I believed him wholeheartedly. I behaved as though he was to be my husband. I was exclusively dating him. I told my mother that I was dating him, and I always disclosed to her whenever I had to meet him. I started staying at his place throughout the night. Many times, I got dressed there, and I went to work from his home. We had a consensual, sexual relationship. Once we embarked upon a second year of secretly dating, I started asking him when he planned to announce that we were dating and planning to be married. He convinced me that everything was fine. He said I should just be patient. My patience was waning once we were approaching a third year of secrecy in dating. I offered him an ultimatum. I told him either he married me, or he would have to stop uncovering me. He said we were doing fine just the way we were. This was the first time I realized that he was utilizing "delaying tactics." Meanwhile, I had received large sums of settlement money in 2006 regarding my home post hurricane Katrina. I was very benevolent with the money when it came to him and the church. I wrote at least three books of checks to him, his church, and his organization. It was all in the name of trust, love, and becoming his future first lady. I wrote several one thousand dollars checks. I wrote a two thousand dollar check when he was about to fly to Africa. I wrote a check to him for five thousand dollars as a gift to help him. All these checks cleared. I paid tithes and innumerable offerings. Everywhere I travelled for the church, I gave and gave. Within a period of three years, I had given close to fifty thousand dollars to him and his church. During the third year of dating him, he made no effort to buy me an engagement ring, so I confronted him a couple more times as to whether he would marry me. I told him I would not be uncovered anymore. He continued to call me for a few months, and I even remained at the ministry. We discontinued the sexual relationship by 2009. From 2009 to the present, I have been celibate. It has been eleven years of celibacy for me. I had a deep love for him, and I knew it would take a long time before I could trust another man again. People did suspect that he and I had been dating. A couple of individuals shared that they had seen him taking me back to my car on certain mornings. I would park my car at nearby places, and he would drive me to his home. Several times he suggested that I just park my car at his home. I declined, because his lady friends had started making comments to me as though they knew he had been seeing me. I had a few arguments with ladies that he was said to have been dating simultaneously. Eventually, people had begun to tell me that he was seeing other women. He was supposedly promising to marry them also. Many of them had purchased wedding gowns in hopes to marry him. I confronted him about one woman in particular who was on his staff. One day I was in his church office with him, and this woman stood outside his door knocking and singing, "You must don't know bout me?" He yelled to her that he was busy. We never spoke of the incident again. Most things were never spoken of again. You were really NEVER allowed to question him, stop by unannounced, or discuss anything with anyone about him. Once I was called into a meeting with the same "staff" woman to alleviate her concerns as to whether he had given me an engagement ring. I said no he hadn't given me a ring, and I went on. One night he called me, and he demanded that I say he and I had not been dating. I did not comply with his wishes. I said he and I had been dating for up to three years secretly. I suspected that he had someone listening on the other line. This is the first time he expressed anger and fury towards me. He was irate…livid even. This was the first time I saw that side of him. It would not be the last. He said I should expect to be called into a meeting that Sunday. I had already made a decision not to attend service that Sunday. I didn't go to church, and I didn't attend another meeting. One of the ladies called me, and she said he was looking all over for me. He called me that evening, and he said don't let guilt keep you away. He had expected me to say we hadn't dated. I had purposed in my heart to tell the truth at all cost. He said he wanted me to remain at the ministry. I told him I would stay, but I would not attend any meeting he'd arrange. I remained at the church, and eventually he stopped calling me. After a few months, he stopped speaking to me altogether. He started throwing slang from the pulpit every service, and this became his battleground. He would say demeaning things. He openly denied ever having any relationship with any woman who ever attended his church. He said all the women were delusional and crazy. I was told by a lady that the leader banged on a table in a private meeting saying, "I have never had anything to do with that woman!! She is delusional and crazy!! (He was referring to me. It was one lie from him after the other.) This lady was someone I confided in about the "entanglement." She told me about past and current involvements with women he was said to have had. Some of these relationships, God had confirmed to me. God showed me dreams and visions as well. He even showed me which women were being uncovered. I later saw these same women leaving his home at all odd hours of the day and night. This was during my many visits to his neighbor, my best friend at the time. Many things I saw with my own two eyes. He said he never asked any of the women for their phone numbers, and he never had any involvement with any of them. He professed to be celibate. I knew that was a great untruth, because we had been sleeping together from 2006 to 2009. He had been divorced more than twenty years when I met him. It was voiced that one of the "staff" women had been seeing him for more than 20 years. This is the woman who gave me the most grief. In some instances she reached out to help me in ministry. However she expressed some ill feelings towards me on other occasions. There were at least four other women I knew he was having relations with. Someone he worked closely with confirmed the leader's sexual involvement with all four of them. These were the same women I saw come and go at his home. All the stories were coinciding. From the pulpit, he spoke of personal things that I knew were regarding he and I. I watched him leave me for the others. Many women came and went. The "core women stayed." There were at least ten that I knew of. I saw things. As I mentioned, I was close friends with one of his neighbors. My friend would confirm to her husband that the leader said things from the pulpit that confirmed he had a relationship with me in the past. There were things I told her, and the leader said them from the pulpit. He had no way of knowing that I had told her everything. My friend saw even more than I did. She would divulge all the information she knew. I can have a lie detector test administered to me to confirm that I definitely had a sexual relationship with him over a span of three years. I kept the dress. At the church, I did have a friend named "Emerald" who guided me through a great deal of the hurt and pain that stemmed from his ultimate betrayal. She and I would pray together frequently. She had seen enough proof to know that he and I had been seeing each other. She was always there as a good friend. We were there for each other in ministry. Were it not for her, it would have been even more difficult to begin to heal. She told me that I would ultimately have to leave in order to completely forget and to heal. She was right. She left the ministry before I left. The mental and verbal abuse, the lies, the manipulation, were all more damaging to me than any physical abuse. He was a master deceiver and a manipulator. To me, it would have been easier to leave if he had been beating me or physically attacking me. There would have been outward proof and signs. Mental and verbal abuse come with subtle or no signs. He never struck me or abused me physically. The effects of mental and verbal abuse are intolerable and long lasting. At times, I was depressed and suicidal even. He tried to make people think I was insane. He tried to make me think I was insane. There were times he could tell me where I had gone throughout the day. He would call and ask if my meeting was over with so and so. I would not have told him whom I had to meet with. There were many times he could tell me where I had been. One night I was in bed with him, and he said the last woman he had to park his truck, walk a distance and follow her, he shot! I didn't take him seriously. However, he did have a gun on the nightstand. I asked him what was he planning to do with it. He said, "Keep being mysterious, you'll find out." My next question was, "Did you go to jail for shooting the woman?" He looked at me, and said, "Don't be concerned about that!" After that night, I never saw the gun again, and I never asked about it. I never believed that he would ever shoot me or hit me. He never did either to me. I was still in love with him at that time, so I would have believed anything he told me. I was expected never to go anywhere near another man. I never did. Except once I had to meet my ex the day after Valentine's Day, 2007. The leader was seeing a new woman who had joined the church, so I vindictively went on one date while I dated the leader. He acted as though he already knew about the interlude, so I confessed to him. He wouldn't talk to me for an entire week. He called once that week, and he was furious. I decided to let him do all the talking, because I knew that was an argument I would never win. Conversely, he was seeing all the women he so desired to see. This is how it was with him. He called me again the end of that week on a Friday. Towards the end of our relationship, Friday was our night. He said, "It's our night. What are you doing? Are you still taking care of your little doctor friend?" I told him no. It was just a dinner date. He was mad!! The next day he returned home, and he called me. He asked if I was coming over. I hesitated, because I didn't know what he would do. He said, "Oh you don't want to see me now?" I told him of course I wanted to see him. There we were again! I went back over there, and he told me he never wanted me to mention that man or the date again, ever. I didn't. You had to do everything he said, how he said, when he said, or it would be nothing nice. I fit right into his "box" he put me in. Once he told me he had a cage upstairs to put me in, since he didn't want me dealing with any other man. I believed he would have done it. Once we were no longer together dating, I heard that he was prone to violence and beat women. He was probably the most powerful speaker I had ever met, and I had traveled all over and heard some of the greatest speakers. He had an even greater anointing than any of them. His voice resonated in your spirit long after the revivals, church services, and church meetings were over. I received miracles through his hands. As much money as I gave, I continued to get blessed with more money. I would give money to the other members. I bought gifts, clothes, suits, computers, a printer, towels, whatever for whomever needed it. I started my own ministry of helps. I did it all from my heart, and I never expected anything in return. Still, I was accused of having a motive and an under current. These were his words. I had already been with him innumerable times, yet I had some ulterior motive. I can't even begin to tell it all. I must share that I was expecting at one time. A pregnancy test was positive, so I planned to see my doctor that Monday. I had been nauseated, vomiting in the early part of the days, fatigued, hungry, and lightheaded. The only time I felt well was when I was around him. On that weekend, I began to bleed incessantly. I drove myself to the ER, and the doctor who examined me said I was having a miscarriage. The doctor said nature had already begun to take its course, so there was nothing that could be done. I was getting accustomed to the idea that I would possibly have a child. On a visit to his home the week before, he asked me what was wrong with me? He asked why are you so tired and doing all this sleeping. I ate popcorn, so I wouldn't be nauseous. He said I never ate much before then. He looked me square in the eyes, and he said, "You think I don't know when something is wrong with you? You are not even going to tell me?" I couldn't tell him. I had planned to go away, and I would have the child without letting him know. I do not have any biological children of my own, so this hit deep to the core. I went into somewhat of a depression for a few months following the incident. Eventually, I healed. I never told him.

I saw two women on separate occasions leave his home around 6:00 am from his garage. I saw a particular staff person who would be at his home for hours on end much like I was there. This lady would stand in the sliding door smiling as if to taunt me. My good friend who would walk the neighborhood with me would see everything I saw. When I dated him, I was at his house many hours at a time. I always spent the night with him. One night a lady showed up banging on his door demanding that he came out. He never answered the door, but we could see her on the cameras. He had surveillance cameras surrounding his home. His bedroom was the only one downstairs, and he had an office that you walked through the bedroom to get to. If you entered the house from the garage, the kitchen was off to the right, a storage closet to the left, den straight ahead, a small bathroom to the left, breakfast area to the right, dining room was near the foyer, the staircase was to the left before you entered his bedroom. All the other bedrooms were upstairs. I counted four. In the center upstairs was a sitting area. I spent all my time with him in his bedroom or den when I was there. He had a patio and swimming pool in the back yard. His house was grand! It was about nine thousand square foot living area. It was somewhat of a castle. I stayed with him for the time I was with him, because I loved him. I trusted him, and I believed in him. He was tall, dark, and handsome. He was cultured, refined, debonair, and he had a certain flare. He dressed just the way I liked. (GQ… Designer suits) His hair was wavy, laid to the back, and perfect. His skin was like caramel. He had pretty teeth, and a great smile. Everything was perfect. He smelled perfect. His shoes were perfect. (Designer) From head to toe, he was perfect. He gave two hundred percent in the bedroom. He had me convinced that he had eyes only for me. He took me out to dinner often at the beginning. He offered to buy me clothes in the beginning. He always asked if I needed anything. He was attentive when I was there with him. He called frequently. When I wasn't with him, we were on the phone talking all night until morning. I would sing to him. When one of us fell asleep, the other person would call back. One month, he stopped all travel plans. We spent all that time together. He would go in to the ministry during the day, and we had plans thereafter everyday. We talked off and on throughout the day. He was gentle, kind, passionate, caring, sensitive, loving, happy, smiling always, settled, and never violent. We never had a disagreement or argument until the second year. During the second year, the only argument we had was whether or not he was dating someone else. On one occasion, I told him I had met with my ex. That didn't turn out well. We got through that, and we resumed a "normal" dating relationship before the ultimate end. The only grievance I had was that I was a secret. For the first two years, everything was almost perfect. He asked me to never leave him, to care for him, love him, and always dance for him. I had begun to be a liturgical dancer then. While we dated, I went to the Bahamas, Jamaica, Hawaii, and Los Angeles. Due to ministry, he said he couldn't get away to take the trips. However, we talked all night and day while I was on the trips. It was so great with us that I never dreamed we wouldn't be married. I believe this is why the end was so devastating. Everything with us was like a fairy tale until we were about to break up. It was months of bliss! It made sense that the church congregation would have to be prepared to receive the lady in waiting. Apparently, this was why his plan worked. He would go on to someone else when he was ready to. He would also continue dating others as well. It became a pattern. After 2009, we never dated again. I danced and traveled to other churches. I spoke at other churches as well. One of the leaders that served him pulled me aside one day, and she told me that I was sworn to secrecy. She said I was never allowed to speak of anything regarding he and I. I rarely spoke of our involvement. Women would come and go. I just watched from a distance. The humiliation, resentment, ostracism, verbal and mental mistreatment didn't commence until we were no longer dating. When I had first met him, he was so anointed. He had the voice of thunder, and I watched as miracles took place, testimonies went forth, and he preached the horns off a Billy goat!!! I didn't see the end coming, because it all seemed so perfect.

Periodically, I would leave and return. Mostly the women connected to him would act snobbish. They would try to act demeaning. I developed a thick skin, and I went straight to "Nutville" on them a couple of times. Once I had invited a good guy friend to service with me. The leader did not handle that well. My friend said he would never return. The leader asked him to call him. They knew one another through business. My friend said the leader told him to watch me, because I was sneaky. The guy said after that conversation, he knew I had been intimately involved with the leader. That friend never returned to the ministry with me. I apologize if this is difficult to follow, but I am being very careful not to mention names. Some people see red flags and signs, but my situation was far from the norm. When I was around him, I was physically well. I smiled all the time. People noticed that I was smiling always. It was as though he and I were the only two in the universe. Either I was brainwashed, or I was in a place like heaven with him. It was all pretentious.

The preliminaries have been presented. On April 21, 2017, the tables really turned. I had actually left the ministry. I was visiting the leader's church for a conference. It was the third night I had gone there, and the meeting was over. I need to set the records straight. I was physically and viciously attacked. I did not have a fight with anyone. Even after being attacked, I did not strike or hit anyone back. Witnesses came forward who attested to this fact. If the lie is still circulating about a fight, I silence the devil right here and right now. I have NEVER fought over a man in my life. I never plan to either. I was approached by men constantly, just as much or more than the leader was approached. The leader and I had been broken up since 2009. At ten o'clock that night, a young girl attacked me, and she started hitting me in the head. I repeat, "It was not a fight! I was viciously attacked!!" I fell backwards, and my body slammed onto the concrete parking lot. I literally felt my back snap. I blacked out for a short while, because I didn't know what happened to my computer, the bag, and my purse. When I regained consciousness, I heard the girl and her group screaming, "Let's finish her off." I clearly heard the Lord say, "The angels of the Lord encampeth around about those that fear Him and delivereth them." I knew then that I would make it safely home. They laughed uncontrollably, and they yelled obscenities. A bishop and one of the dancers I had danced previously with helped me back into the sanctuary. One of the female pastors threatened to punch me in the face. She kept coming towards me. She was cursing, and she acted like a crazy, wild person. The assistant pastor, the leader's son, ran out to tell me not to call the police. He said if I called the police I could forget about ever returning on the grounds again. I told him I was the one who was attacked. I let him know I would call the police, and I would be happy never to return to the grounds. I called the police especially since they were all saying they would further attack me. The police arrived about five minutes later. They took my statement, asked me if I wanted to press charges, and the police went into the sanctuary to locate the perpetrators. I did press charges. The police were told that the girl and the others had already left the premises. I had a couple of witnesses who gave statements to the police on my behalf. The church administrator, "Mary" came outside where the attack had taken place, and she turn her body completely around, so she wouldn't offer any assistance. I knew she was involved with leader intimately, so I didn't expect any help from her. Her brother offered to give a statement to the police on my behalf, but "Mary" advised him not to. The police ruled the incident in my favor as simple battery. They said they would make another attempt to have the girl arrested. The individuals were from another state, so this would be a difficult task. Until this day, no arrests were ever made. The leader, nor any of the governing Pastors ever apologized to me until this day. I went to the ER the following day. I took pictures of my injuries. My face was red, purple, and blue. I had three huge contusions on my forehead. I had bruises, scrapes, scratches from head to toe especially of the left side of my body. I had a severe headache. My body ached everywhere. My left ankle was twisted. My neck was injured. My entire back ached. My left shoulder was extremely sore. My right and left hips were injured. It felt as though a truck had run over me. At the ER the nurse took pictures of my injuries. I had X-rays done, CT scan of the brain (Due to brain tumor history), and a thorough exam. The nurse asked if I had reported the domestic event to the police. The staff thought it was a domestic violence incident. I explained to them what had occurred. It was confirmed that I had a concussion, contusions, rotator cuff injury, left ankle sprain, hematomas, and generalized pain, and post traumatic stress disorder. I was referred to a center where I could begin therapy for my neck, back, and left shoulder. I remained in therapy for over a month, but the doctor there decided I needed an emergency MRI of my spine. The pain was worsening in my back every visit, and I needed to utilize a back brace to move about. It was suspected that there was extensive structural damage to my back. An MRI would later show severe damage to L3, L4, L5, and S1. There was bulging of the disc with posterior annular fissuring L4-L5 along with severe left and moderate to severe right facet arthropathy. The findings showed moderate right facet arthropathy L5-S1 with mild annular bulging and posterior annular fissuring. There was left and posterolateral outer annular fissuring L3-L4 with annular bulging. Clinical history shows results are after an assault. Before the assault, I never had any back injury or head injury. I also had a diagnosis of piriformis syndrome. There was a diagnosis of sacroiliac joint dysfunction of the right side, myofascial pain, I could no longer sleep on my right side or back. I had a limp on the right side for months. I used pain creams, pain patches, over the counter medication everyday for at least four months, because I have never been able to take narcotics. For the first four months, the pain was intense. On a scale of one to ten, ten being the highest, the pain was an eleven. I had at least three more trips to the ER with debilitating pain. On the last trip, I could not even put one foot in front the other. Eventually, surgery or facet injections were recommended. The physical Medicine and Rehabilitation doctor told me that my lower back deviated to the right. He said it looked as though I had scoliosis. I have never been diagnosed with scoliosis, and I had never had previous injuries such as these. The same doctor told me that I was injured far more than I could have realized. He said I could have been killed out there that night.

I had someone to send correspondence to the leader of the organization, so we could obtain insurance information. No information was ever sent or released. I had no other alternative but to seek legal counsel. The lawyer was never successful in getting any phone number or address of the insurance company that insured the churches' property. I officially filed the lawsuit a year later which was within the statute of limitations guidelines. Only after I filed the lawsuit was the insurance information released to me. It was too late to just file an insurance claim. At that time, I was only being advised by an attorney. The lawyer requested video footage which was in fact available. The Gonzales Police department attempted to meet someone at the church to obtain the video footage, but they were given the runaround by the staff and leader. It was all handled as a "joke" to these individuals. The leader was connected to the mayor, the police, parish officials, and more. He seemed to have absolutely no remorse. He acted as though he was above the law. I had texted him in March 2017 about the threats from the ladies in question, and he denied that I had sent any texts. I received no compensation from the churches' insurance company. I was the one grilled and put on trial by the lawyers who victimized me all over again. I was kept in a deposition six and a half hours. I told the truth, and the lawyer asked me the same questions repeatedly about 20 times. It was nothing short of a nightmare. I was out of work for months. I had nightmares of the attack. My sleeping pattern was altered. The attack originated because of an Apostle who didn't want to be referred to by her first name. I uploaded a post on my page that stated, "When you leave a church or an organization, expect lies to be made up about you." The apostle in question sent me a message to demand that I remove the post from my page. I replied to her promptly, and I informed her that I would not be removing the post. It was my personal page. I referred to her as "Ophelia." She notified her daughter, the pastor who yelled and screamed obscenities the night I was attacked. This Pastor sent me a message also stating that I should be slapped for calling her mother by her first name. This Pastor was said to have had a child for the leader's son. That's a whole story by itself. I was not even a part of the organization any more. I did not owe her anything. I was not referring to her by any title. This was the same Pastor who threatened to punch me in the face and beat me. She also informed her granddaughter who later physically attacked me. The granddaughter also sent me a threatening message saying that she would attack me the next time she saw me. It was March of 2017 when the threats came, and I texted the leader to let him know what the ladies were planning to do. I also informed others, including the leader's mother who was a friend of mine. His mother called me. She said her son said he'd handle the matter. No one would be coming to his church property to attack anyone. Of course, the young lady attacked me on the property of his church a month later. The leader was well aware of what was planned. The attack was premeditated. The law supposedly protects these individuals, and they are allowed to attack anyone they desire to on anyone's property. I can appeal the decision, but I would need a lawyer who would actually be proactive in fighting the case. I feel that my lawyer was passive. She just waited to hear from the opposing lawyers, put some statements together, and waited some more. I had to attend two depositions alone even after I had an attorney of record. I had to make a valiant attempt to fight to get my medical bills paid at least. Nothing was ever paid. God, however is still taking care of me.

Despite the fact that I had no back surgery or facet injections as recommended by the doctors, I can still do my liturgical dances. I walk on my treadmill also, but I use my back brace while doing so.

Before I conclude this chapter, I must add a few more things I was subjected to. I will conclude the narrative section with a final chapter before the devotional sections. In the inspirational section you will see poetry, scriptural affirmations, and daily inspirations and motivation. The first part of this book is "raw" and "real." I have finally displayed the courage and the stamina to tell my story to the world without reservation or inhibitions, rhyme, or reason. I lived in a land of extremes. There was actually no "normalcy" in the organization. The same "Ophelia" stood in front of me once while she was preaching and said, "What's happened to you? You are not as pretty any more. You've gained weight! You need to do better!" I had gained the fifty pounds, and I was still undergoing treatment for the brain tumor. I started crying, and a lady got up to comfort me. "Ophelia" told her to sit down, and let God break me all the way down. I needed to go lose some weight she said. Granted, today I have lost over sixty pounds, and I have kept them off. As far as I am concerned, I have always looked better than her on my worst day. It had to be the holy spirit that constrained me from telling her off right then and there. The person I used to be would have let her have it. That evening, there was another service. I showed up wearing the exact same clothes and everything on purpose. She had the audacity to speak to me, and I kept on walking like she was the wrong street. She preached again, and talked about how the women from BR just needed to do better with their appearance, hair, clothes, makeup, etc. She even said, "Some of y'all look like y'all haven't had sex for years. At least look like you are having some." I never spoke to her again. She bought the leader a Bentley the year before I left the organization. One night she gave $10,000.00 in the offering. She always bought him suits, expensive gifts, etc. Other ladies reported that this lady came against them, and she even roughed a few people up. The leader never sat her down. She was one of his meal tickets. She was married to a man from the Islands who was about thirty years plus younger than her. This lady and her entourage went for bad. There was a lady who was said to have taken a second mortgage out on her home to give the leader a big check. Many women showered him with clothes, shoes, gifts, money. You name it, they gave it to him. For his anniversary every year, we were expected to give him a thousand dollars. If you didn't give the money, you would be mistreated even more. Some people just left the organization if they couldn't give the money. One year, "Ophelia" said everyone should give their income tax check to the leader. Some gave it. I didn't, and I was treated worse. I could say a lot more here, but I will leave it at that. "Ophelia" and her group lived in another state as I stated earlier. Once the leader and I had broken up, he made my life a living nightmare. He turned most of the people against me. He ridiculed me, laughed at me, overlooked me, acted like I was the devil himself. I would dance solo liturgical dances in his church, and so many people would shout, dance, run, and be blessed. He would get in the pulpit, and he would act like I was a demon. He would say, "Why are you jealous of a dancer? She could be a dancing devil!" The people would laugh, and he would laugh. It was all about mind games and spiritual manipulation. Then he would preach for you to stay. He would say, your greatest humiliation is your greatest elevation. He would always say something to make you hold on and not leave. Once he said, "Deep down inside, I don't want you to leave!" I would always text him when I was ready to leave the organization. Sometimes, I left service early and crying. A few times, I left the ministry, but I would always go back. The ladies he was seeing would get all the promotions, the elevations, titles, sermons, preferential treatment, and bonuses. I saw them as his concubines. I saw the organization as a cult. I saw him as the leader of the occult. He was a master manipulator. He paid some of the ladies' bills. I witnessed him tell a couple of them that he would pay their car insurance. He helped them to buy cars also. It is not my desire to disclose too much, but taking you deep into what was going on is necessary. Just as good as it was in the beginning, it was the worst experience of my life in the end. I was sat down at any given time for anything. His ladies could do worse, and he would never sit them down. By the time I left there, my self esteem had plummeted down to an all time low. I fought for my salvation. I actually hated him at one point. I prayed for forgiveness. I had to learn to accept the apology I would never get. This man had no remorse. He acted as though he was perfect, and he did no wrong. I told him once that I regretted he day I ever met him, and I did at the time. There is a thin line between love and hate. When I first sat down to write the narratives for this book, I kept it sweet. I was docile, and I was passive even. I believe it was to signify my healing. It really doesn't hurt anymore. I definitely don't love him anymore. I say, "Father forgive them, for they know not what they do." The strongholds, and the chains are now broken off my life. It is my earnest desire that someone is set free from that same bondage. I pray that someone is saved and delivered from the pain of their past.

THE FINAL CHAPTER:

God, Set someone free!

I shared my story, because I want others to encounter deliverance and salvation in the very same areas that I was held captive in. God, free someone from the occult! I wrote under an anointing and divine inspiration. I actually excluded as much as I could. This is the sanitized version. It was necessary to share the depth of my encounters and experiences. I went through to pull someone else to. When the anointing lifted, I progressed to the final chapter. I conclude by summoning the hurting men and women who are victims of their daunting past. You can be free today. Emerge from the shadows of uncertainty and the valley of indifference, and indecisiveness. Fight for your salvation at all cost! Forgive, internalize your healing, and let go of the past hurt, pain, and affliction. If you remember nothing else, please apply these truths in dating and marriage

My 10 dating truths:

1. Under no circumstances should anyone date someone secretly or in the dark.
2. If someone promises to marry you, and you are never given a ring, most likely he will not marry you.
3. If God doesn't tell you to wait years for someone to marry you, do not wait. If a man or woman is dating anybody else while dating you, it is not God.
4. Pray fervently before making the decision to date or to marry anyone.
5. Do not remain a part of any church or organization if the leader is lying about his involvements, especially if you know he was involved with you.
6. Once God reveals all, believe Him! If God tells you to leave, leave!! God began to reveal many things, and he offered me many premonitions. I ignored some of the signs.
7. Take full responsibility of your role in the circumstances, and purpose in your heart never to make the same decisions again.
   I take full responsibility for the choices I made. I learned this lesson the hard way. No one deserves to be treated as a dirty secret.
8. Forgive yourself! Forgive those who hurt you.
9. Fight for your salvation. Stay in the word.
10. Love yourself no matter what. You deserve to be happy, whole, and free.

If I could have a word with the leader of the organization on today, I would admonish him to free his daughters and sons from any bondage that is not of God. I beseech him to release them now in the name of Jesus! Loose your hold on them, and let them go. Please choose just one woman to marry, and free the remainder of them! Be true to yourself. Be true to others. Don't use people. Apologize to those you hurt. Repent for your own sins, and get it right with God. Forgive me if I hurt you in any way. I forgive you for all you did to me. I accept your apology even if you are not sorry. I'm free! Good-bye.

Now, I fully embrace my calling. I truly believe I am called and chosen by God to walk in the office of an Apostle. I am on a divine assignment to assist those who are hurting from the wounds of their past. If you are healing from a broken relationship, suicidal tendencies, or a low self esteem, I am your levitical priest. God sent me here to stand in the gap on your behalf. I was affirmed as an Apostle on September 9, 2018. I became the Senior Pastor of my church on the same day. I received my first doctorate of Divinity from American F.C. on March 4, 2018. I served at church on Fire of Gonzales, Louisiana for about five months under the instruction of my overseer at that time who was Apostle Dr. G. E. I founded and established Divine Deliverance International Outreach Ministries in September 2018. In April 2020, I was set to receive a second Doctorate of Divinity from St. Thomas Christian University. Due to the Pandemic and the escalating cases of Covid 19, the spring ceremony was postponed. The new date was set for August 22, 2020. I was scheduled to walk with the fall class 2020.

I want to take this time to share information about my two television shows. The first show as I stated earlier was on the Now Television Network. It was entitled, "Mindset for Miracles!" On my very first show, I talked about my platform being a message of inspiration, encouragement, and empowerment. The first message was the "pacesetter" for the broadcasting series. The show aired at 9:00am Eastern standard time on Mondays. I opened with, "Get ready for a "mind transforming" word encounter that defied the laws of normalcy and transcended them! You'll be propelled into a realm of the spirit that catapults you to a higher dimension! Allow God to put a "super" to your natural!

Philippians 2:5 " Let this mind be in you which is also in Christ Jesus.

Once you condition your mind, you change your thinking. KJV

Proverbs 23:7 "For as a man thinketh, so is he."KJV

If you are ready to acquire an even greater mindset for miracles, this broadcast is for you. As we develop an even greater intimacy with God, we can surrender ourselves completely and unreservedly to him.

Miracles are things that are inexplicable, mystifying, divine interventions in human affairs.

Mindset: beliefs held by people or groups of people. An established set of attitudes.

(I shared personal testimonies of miracles I received.)

My first subject on the first show was:

Subject: "Journey with me through Gethsemane!"

Your miracle is on the other side of:
1. Humility
2. The dark place
3. Lowliness in mind
4. Compassion
5. Divine nature
6. Meekness
7. Valleys

Be willing to walk through Gethsemane!

Jesus prayed when huge drops of sweat fell from him like blood. It was similar to hematidrosis, the process in which drops of blood come through the pores of the skin. The condition is due to extreme emotional distress.

Luke 22:44 "And being in an agony he prayed more earnestly: and his sweat was as drops of blood falling down from the ground." KJV

Jesus suffered and agonized. His close friends couldn't stay up and pray with him. Jesus prayed alone. He endured false accusations, trumped up charges, humiliation, mocking, being spit on, lied on, beatings, strikes, scourging, (whippings causing His flesh to be ripped open). He carried a cross in front of mocking crowds. He wore a crown of thorns. He was crucified, and He carried the sins of the world. Hence, originated the plan of salvation. If a reader wants to be saved right now, I can lead you to Christ. Tell the Lord you are sorry for your sins. Ask Him to forgive you for your sins.

Confess Romans 10:9,10 KJV

9 That if thou shalt confess with thy mouth the Lord Jesus, and shalt believe in thine heart that God raised him from the dead, thou shalt be saved.

10 For with the heart man believeth unto righteousness; and with the mouth confession is made unto salvation.

Now, you are saved! I am rejoicing with you! You are a partaker of God's divine inheritance!

The miracle is in the instructions, follow the instructions, and you will get your miracle! I free flow at the end of all my messages, so this concludes the very first television message I preached. I am no longer broadcasting on this Network.

I am now still on Preach the Word Worldwide Network television, and the show airs every Monday through Friday at 4:30pm central time. I would love for you to tune in, or watch the show on demand. You can check www.PTWWNTV.COM for television distribution. My first message on "Activate your faith!" is here:

I heard a sound from the heavens saying, "Receive His glory!" In all of His excellency, He's pouring out more of His glory! I give Him all the glory, honor, and adoration due unto His name. He's my keeper, my joy, my future, and the love of my life! I extend accolades to the visionary, Apostle Dr. Marilyn Todman and Bishop Charles Todman, CEOs and Founders of Preach the Word Worldwide Network Television. I am forever grateful to God and these anointed, appointed, powerful, highly favored, better than blessed, and divinely assigned people of God!

(Scriptural Affirmations)

Subject: The waters are troubled!

What does it mean to activate your faith? (To cause to operate, to initiate, to generate, to cause to function, to be proactive in the realm of the spirit, to catapult, to set it off…) God may require something of us before we receive the miracle, the blessing, the healing, the promotion, the financial miracle… It's like receiving a new car. The car can't drive itself. We have to get in, start it up, and drive! If we follow the instructions, we will get the miracle!

In the field of chemistry:

Reactants----------$\rightarrow$ >>>>>>>>>>>>> Products

(catalyst or inhibitors)

The catalyst causes the reaction to move forward. The inhibitors are antagonistic to the forward movement of the products. We need some spiritual catalyst to propel others into their destiny!

In the field of Physics, we were taught that in order for there to be a sound, there must be a recipient of the sound. In the spirit realm, it works in a similar fashion. "So then, faith cometh by hearing, and hearing by the word of God." Romans 10:17 We've all heard so much word that we should believe what God says. I hear a sound from the heavens resonating from my spirit! Your latter will be greater than your past!! Somebody ought to shout with the voice of triumph!!!

John 5:1-8 (A lame man at the pool of Bethesda waited 38 years for a healing. He was complacent in a dark place. He didn't ask anyone to put him in the water, so he could be healed. He found excuses. He said every time he tried to get in the water, someone would get in before him.) When you are needing a miracle, it calls for desperation many times!!! I don't know about you, but I would have rolled, crawled, slid, whatever it took!!!!! Be determined to receive your miracle at all cost! "Activate Your Faith!!"

In kingdom service, I am Apostle Dr. Julie Jones, Senior Pastor of Divine Deliverance International Outreach Ministries. This book was written under divine instruction and revelation. In my flesh, I didn't want to do it! I had to humble myself, and I had to become transparent. This is spiritual. I went through this for the masses of hurt men and women who encountered pain much like I did. You can get over it! You can learn to live without shame, guilt, and misunderstanding! You can heal, and you can facilitate the healing and deliverance of others! My Bio is included on the back cover. Much Life! Much Love! Muah

SECTION TWO:

POETRY, DAILY INSPIRATION AND MOTIVATION!

Music in My Heart....

A tender heart dancing, leaping beyond measure…

Encompassed with a song… my joy… a golden treasure…

A melody so familiar it,

Keeps my heart beating….

Echoing sounds of yesterday… enlightening and completing…

The harmony of love piercing through my soul…

Through rhythmical verses,

I could clearly see my goal.

Finding the sweet forever even from the start.

Jesus is the man who put the music in my heart.

Alabaster Box...

This precious box I carry, no one knows the cost.

Now saved, once a sinner and lost…

No more guilt, shame or condemnation…

It's all erased upon salvation!

Accepted of Christ.... rejected as well.... a paradox.

You don't know what I paid for this precious alabaster box.

This is my praise and my dance unto the Master.

Luke 7:37:38 KJV

37 And, behold, a woman in the city, which was a sinner, when she knew that Jesus was at meat in the Pharisee's house, brought an alabaster box of ointment,
38 And stood at His feet behind Him weeping, and began to wash His feet with tears, and did wipe them with the hairs of her head, and kissed his fee, and anointed them with ointment.

Sparkle in my eyes...

Special Dedication: From my heart…
God, I thank you for allowing me to see another year.
God in His infinite wisdom created me to be the woman I have become.
He has dealt emphatically with me.
I am single, saved, sanctified, and satisfied. I am God's up and coming, recently released, chosen and called like Esther for such a time as this. I am a woman of purpose and destiny. I am created for the master's use. Yes, I am so in love with the Lord!

Sparkle in My Eyes…

This sparkle in my eyes caught me by surprise.
For now I realize that in time, I've grown wise.
I smile even after the sighs, smiles, and cries.
My how time flies, I no longer have the girlish hips and thighs.
I'm living in an era where chaos is on the rise!
For trials have made me a queen. To my King, I'm His prize.
I'm not my little girlish size, but I'm wise... a queen, the King's prize.

Living Sacrifice: To the Master...

(My first original song I wrote)

Everything, and all that I am,

I surrender to you.

I yield every part of me...

Everything I do.

I give my life, my love, joy, and sorrow.

Lord, I give you today... my future and my tomorrow.

I'm your living sacrifice.

I'm your living sacrifice.

Everything I am and hope to be. I surrender to you Jesus... all you gave to me. My body is yours holy, acceptable, bought with a price. I present my body as a living sacrifice.

In my life, I've seen sorrow and pain, but you brought sunshine after the rain. You held me in your arms, and wiped every tear, away. I'm your living sacrifice.

Today and everyday, I pledge my mind, my heart, and body to you. I yield every part of me, everything I do.

My body is yours, holy, acceptable bought with a price. I present my body as a living sacrifice.

Up tempo (Living Sacrifice)

Living sacrifice…

Bought by a price…

God gave His… son to die for me…

He gave His… life to set us free…

I'm Holy… acceptable in His sight.

God gave His… son to die for me.

He gave His… life to set us free.

I am a living sacrifice...

Well, you ought to rejoice.

You ought to shout.

God's saving grace has brought you out.

The price was paid on Calvary's Hill.

He gave us power to do His will.

I give Him my life!

I was bought by a price.

His love made me a living sacrifice!

Living Sacrifice!

Living Sacrifice! I am a living sacrifice!

Eagle

I am the eagle ~ soaring to greater heights…

Unlimited boundaries…

Blue skies laced with opportunities unexplored…

For I am meek, and yet, I am strong.

Hear the music of my heart!

Oh, the sweet, sweet song…

I sing of the mountains

climbed, and of the rivers

I have crossed!

I sing for "our people".

Our hopes must not be lost.

This eagle shall sing her songs, and fly above each boundless sea!

She shall sing with sweet, sweet music.

For through Jesus Christ she is free!

Greater Heights

(Know who you are in God...)

I am the future... partaking of freedom's fountain!

Immovably I stand, secured

to freedom's mountain.

The dreamer awakening to a newfound reality…

Capable of attaining the ultimate in me…

Destined to achieve all that I aspire...

Driven by yesterday's dreamer

who lit the eternal fire…

Waving the torch of peace and brotherhood that freedom's flame ignites…

I am the eagle, living the dream... Soaring to greater heights!

June 3, 2020 Special Dedication:

* 53rd Birthday *

A vital part of my testimony is that so many people have shared that I look as though I'm in my 30s. Even after threatening brain surgery twice, recovery from peripheral vision loss, threats of possible breast cancer for the last four years, I'm still here!

On my 53rd birthday, I'm grateful to God today for starting the second year of my broadcast on "Preach the World Worldwide Network Television. The broadcast is entitled, "Activate your Faith!" The show airs Monday through Friday at 4:30pm central time. (PTWWNTV.COM)

Higher Realm of Expectancy...

Beautiful memories have arisen. The mind is plagued with unscathed thought.

All have emerged from the tranquility I sought.

Now my King, the master cultivates my intellect.

I have never been alone now that I see retrospect.

He gave such a sweet embrace and a gentle touch.

The times with Christ, my King are treasured so much.

Now, I celebrate. I rejoice in being me. The new horizon birthed a higher realm of expectancy.

Psalm 139:14 "I will praise thee; for I am fearfully and wonderfully made: Marvellous are thy works; and that my soul knoweth right well." KJV

Delays are not denials!

I am commissioned to encourage on a daily basis

In the midst of a desert,

God can bring an oasis.

God can do what He wants without anyone's permission.

He doesn't need a reason or a particular condition.

Stay optimistic even in trials

Delays are not denials!

Isaiah 59:19 KJV So shall they fear the name of the Lord from the west, and His glory from the rising of the sun. When the enemy shall come in like a flood, the Spirit of the Lord shall lift up a standard against him.

God never sleeps!

Every promise He makes, He keeps.

Scriptural Affirmations: "Call unto me, and I will answer thee, and show thee great and mighty things, which thou knowest not." Jeremiah 33:3 KJV

"Behold, I will do a new thing; now it shall spring forth; shall ye not know it? I will even make a way in the wilderness, and rivers in the desert." Isaiah 43:19 KJV

Daily inspiration and motivation: Your struggle has an expiration date! Soon, you'll realize, it was worth the wait! Go on, and celebrate! God does His best work when we think it's too late! God said to tell somebody, "I'm still going to do it!" That dream, that career, that ministry, that business, that promotion, that miracle, that house, that car… God is still going to do it!!

Love Affair with the Lord...

Jesus, there's no man quite like you!

You cleave to the soul like the rose to the morning dew.

You embrace the heart and fulfill me too.

I'm convinced there's no man quite like you.

There's nothing like the comfort of touching you.

How amazing it is to love and be loved by you.

No man enchants me the way you do.

I'm convinced, there's no man quite like you!

There's no greater comfort than holding you.

My, how you whisper love songs old and new.

No man completes me the way you do.

You're majestic and mystifying too!

Who wouldn't pursue one who's so true?

In perilous times this love affair guides me through.

I'm convinced, there's no man quite like you!

Friendship in You....

Our pathways collided, and a figure came into view.

Beyond the gleaming sunset, I saw the image of you.

We became inseparable, our worlds became one.

The laughs, the struggles, the joy,

It was all so much fun.

The times we share are special!

The memories will never die!

In you, I've found a friend.

It's always difficult to say good-bye.

The good times were plentiful.

The bad times were few.

I'll never forget how I found, a special friendship in you.

Heavenly Grandeur.....

The dew drops kissed God's morning light,

And made your eyes so gleaming bright.

Rose petals gathered to caress a smile of gold that heaven had blessed.

What a joy... a treasure... a beautiful friend...

A vibrant spirit embracing the wind…

An eagle gracefully soaring with wings of love…

Lacing the blue skies, appearing as a dove…

A labourer worthy of "the calling" and reward

Anointed and blessed by the Saviour and Lord…

A healing presence of love so fervent…

A child of God, the King's precious servant…

Though I've known you briefly, still, I know you well.

For the glow of Christ within you does eternally dwell…

Oh the heavenly grandeur of your beauty, tender and true…

My friend, you're a joy, I dearly love you.

Painting of You...

Like a dream, I walked onto a canvas, searching the world anew.

I searched for a different setting that soon brought me to you.

A joy so unique it brings sunshine through a storm…

Through Christ, it brings much hope, and in the cold, it keeps me warm.

I continued my journey. My heart said, Paint on.

The true colors came into view in the portrait I had drawn.

Pure innocence and delight were seen just shining through.

A friendship so priceless, such beauty in you…

From the first acquaintance, the feelings came piercing through.

A new beginning, new hope is seen in this portrait of you.

A Mother's Day Tribute

My beautiful, highly, favored, anointed, and blessed Mom... She rocks! She's a tower of strength. She's a confidante, a dearest friend. Her love has made a remarkable difference. God, thank you for giving us such an angel...

The woman called Mother!

She sacrificed, and she offered unlimited advice.

Always, she put our needs before her own.

Whenever she is with us, we never feel alone.

This virtuous woman, so Godly, deserves her flowers.

Without bragging, it's just so difficult to explain this mother of ours.

She's like no other!

She's the beautiful woman we love, called mother!

Proverbs 31:28 "Her children arise up, and call her blessed; her husband also, and he praiseth her." KJV

Fight On!

Visions, dreams ~ a future seemingly shattered…

Enemies and foes ~ somehow flattered…

A heart of gold ~ bleeding and battered…

A countenance seized ~ torn and tattered…

Memories residing … goals scattered…

A soul fights on as though nothing mattered…

The equipped, the enlightened, and the inspired...

Treasures of the soul and spirit bring us the promise of success.

Precious jewels adorned about our necks we find that we possess...

Pearls of wisdom to decipher all things once unknown...

Giving birth to the golden knowledge we can now call our own...

The investment in understanding secures the purchase of (unscathed) thought.

Emeralds of truth, rubies of mercy, and diamonds of grace we have bought.

We find ourselves equipped for the pursuit of greater manifestation.

We're prepared to meet every challenge on this day of elevation.

My dear friends live your dreams as you awaken to each greater height.

We are tomorrow's gold bearing the learner's light.

We perish not for we envision all that we aspire.

We find ourselves enlightened forever reaching higher.

To those who have walked this way, you've inspired me too.

It's a joy to be in Christ! We're equipped, enlightened, and inspired!

When you're moving towards the new, still one yearns for yesterday.

We must purpose in our hearts to enjoy each new today!

Peering towards the future, again shall we walk this way.

Keep us close at heart as we travel the distant miles.

We'll keep in mind this moment that we now encompass with smiles.

We've grown, we've learned, and prospered; today we'll keep you near.

In times to come, we'll remember the joy we've found here.

On the distant tomorrow,

We'll return and reunite.

We'll recapture all the joys and sweet sorrows of tonight.

Our pathways may never again collide on the distant sands of tomorrow.

The memories of everyone will still live within us. Happiness we'll never have to borrow.

Now cheerful hellos of yesterday are transformed into bleak "good-byes."

Still, we shall see you all through opaque, but loving eyes.

Dedication to Mother.....

Mother...

The driving force beneath which kept me flying on....

She's the "Wind beneath my wings" even when I'm gone.

It brings me sweet joy even when I'm crying

She cradles me with warmth when life's sunshine is dying...

It keeps me in love with me, though sometimes, I feel alone.

Seeing my human faults...knowing that in Christ, I've grown...

She inspired me to fight at the times, I felt defeated.

I'm given new inspiration until each task is completed.

Holding me close, yet, from a distance seeing me soar...

Far above the clouds knowing that I shall attain more...

Watching me, sometimes in silence yet saying so much...

Through healing words of wisdom or just a simple touch...

It's the force that guides me like no other.

When I turned around, I saw it was, my darling Mother!

To: Mother

Wings of her Prayers...

It's a miracle from God!

I'm here, still alive.

I'm aspiring to reach my goals, still struggling to survive.

In the midst of desolation I'm finding tranquility and peace.

God told someone to hold my hand... the blessings did increase.

Loneliness at times, prevailed. I had to keep on praying.

Joy did abound; the burdens never dismaying.

Sweet solitude is mine though it leaves me sometimes alone...

Someone feels my pain.

Innumerable sacrifices she's shown.

In a distant place... a seemingly far away land...

God blessed me with an angel on earth. She's holding my hand.

She's right here by my side.

In her presence it's a great joy always to abide.

Still surviving, what a miracle.

I know she forever cares.

Momma always carries me on the wings of her prayers.

Daily Devotions to Last a Lifetime...

God orchestrated the assignment.

He ordered the refinement.

Process of our refinement....

It was to make you.

It was never intended to break you.

God knows exactly what you can handle

What He establishes, no one can dismantle.

We can focus on our assignments.

We mustn't focus on the process of our refinement.

James 1:12 KJV

"Blessed is the man that endureth temptation: for when He is tried, he shall receive the crown of life, which the Lord hath promised to them that love him."

Look at the solution.

There's always a resolution.

Scriptural Affirmations:

12 "Beloved think it not strange when the fiery trials come to try you, as though some strange thing happened unto you:"

13 "But rejoice, in asmuch as ye are partakers of Christ's sufferings; that, when his glory shall be revealed, ye may be glad also with exceeding joy."

1st Peter 4:12,13 KJV

Daily Inspiration and Motivation:

With every temptation, God always shows you a way of escape. You've been tried in the furnace of affliction. Go on through the fire! God is with you every step of the way! He will always accompany you! You will never be alone! Trust God in all things! Nothing comes before God by accident or chance. God is fully aware of every circumstance.

Metamorphosis is here....
Change shall appear....

The cocoon becomes a beautiful butterfly of vivid colors we know.

The rosebud becomes a gorgeous rose that keeps the heart aglow.

We shall become the masterpiece as we follow God's instruction.

No devil, we're not perfect, but we are under construction.

Once we are changed, our new season will not be missed.

This is your time. It's your metamorphosis!

Philippians 1:6 KJV "Being confident of this very thing that he who has begun a good work in you shall perform it until the day of Jesus Christ."

The enemy can't touch this.

We are under (construction).

It's our metamorphosis.

Scriptural Affirmations:

"You are His workmanship, created in Christ Jesus unto good works."

Ephesians 2:10 KJV

'The Lord will perfect that which concerneth me: thy mercy oh Lord endureth forever: forsake not the work of thine own hands." Psalm 138:8 KJV

Daily Inspiration and Motivation:

You are somebody in Christ. God knows about your flaws, imperfections, and accomplishments. Someone says, "You aren't anointed enough, powerful enough, committed enough, faithful enough, or deep enough!" God decided. He doesn't need my opinion, your opinion, neither their opinion! God doesn't look at the outward man. He is concerned about the heart! His vote is the vote you need to succeed. Rely on Him wholeheartedly. You need the Shekinah glory. You can change atmospheres when you enter a room.

Kings and Queens are now on the scene

(You are royalty!)

Wings of the Master....

Yesterday is but a memory in the snapshot of one's mind.

Tomorrow offers promise of the rarest kind.

Trade not the future quests for yesteryears brief interludes.

Exhilarating bliss awaits much like the spirit exudes.

Shed no more tears for the same place that gripped her with disaster.

She dwells in the secret place under the wings of the Master.

Psalm 65:11 "Thou crownest the year with thy goodness; and thy paths drop fatness." KJV

Let Him carry you on His wings!

Always be in expectancy of the greatest things!

Scriptural Affirmations:

"But ye are a chosen generation, a royal priesthood, an holy nation, a peculiar people; that ye should shew forth the praises of Him who hath called you out of darkness into His marvelous light;" 1st Peter 2:9 KJV

Daily Inspiration and Motivation:

One day we can say I have fought a good fight. You are a child of the most high King. You are sons and daughters of the King of Kings! That means you have a royal inheritance! You have a crown of righteousness prepared for you! Keep on marching forward in the things of God! Straighten those crowns Kings and Queens! The other side will be quite grand!!!!

God has need of you.
The labourers are few....

Kingdom building...

There's a special place in the kingdom for you that God orchestrated.

You were designed and purposed for this place for which you were created.

The greater the hurdles are, the greater the transition.

The place to seek is your rightful position.

Remain steadfast and unyielding. It's all about souls and kingdom building.

Matthew 9:37 KJV "Then saith He unto His disciples, the harvest truly is plenteous, but the labourers are few;"

Arrive at your destination! Let there be no contemplation.

Scriptural Affirmations:

"And he saith unto them, Follow me, and I will make you fishers of men." Matthew 4:19

"And they straightway left their nets, and followed him." Matthew 4:20

Daily Inspiration and Motivation:

God is just looking for a yes.

He always does the rest.

God grooms us throughout our journey. It is our obligation, to pray, read the Bible, praise, worship, and submit to God. We must present our bodies as living sacrifices. God honors our obedience. We can trust Him with our life.

Never Let Go!

This journey with the Lord intrigues me so.

There are ups and downs surely you know.

I've laughed, cried, shouted, and sighed.

There's been brokenness, and I've had times with "Godly pride."

Through the tears the fears, and unrelenting hope, we grow.

It was worth it all and my friend, STAND! Never let go!

(Nothing shall separate me from the love of God.)

Hebrews 11:6 KJV

"But without faith, it is impossible to please Him, for He that cometh to God must believe that He is and that He is a rewarder of them that diligently seek Him."

Faith prepares the way for us to have what we say!

Scriptural Affirmations:

"Faith cometh, by hearing, and hearing by the Word of God." Romans 10:17 KJV

"Faith is the substance of things hoped for and the evidence of things not seen."

Hebrews 11:1 KJV

"(As it is written, I have made thee a father of many nations,) before whom he believed, even God, who quickeneth the dead, and calleth those things which be not as though they were." Romans 4:17 KJV

Daily Inspiration and Motivation:

Just step out on faith, God will meet you there. Don't concede to the kingdom of darkness. If God promised it, He'll deliver it. Sarah judged Him faithful who promised! You can do the same. God delights in delivering the blessing to you. Keep moving towards destiny!

God designed us to be tenacious, and resilient.

We serve an amazing God who's more than brilliant.

Faith makes us diligent!

The word makes us soldiers with great militance.

The safest place to be is in the will of God.

Satisfaction guaranteed...

There's a place in God where nothing else matters but pursuing His will.

It's the safest place when we realize it's what we must fulfill.

You'll find the place where we acknowledge God in every word or deed.

Then, you embark upon the path marked, "Satisfaction Guaranteed!"

Colossian 3:17 KJV "And whatsoever ye do in word or deed, do all in the name of the Lord Jesus, giving thanks to God and the Father by him."

There's safety in the will. Needs are fulfilled.

Scriptural Affirmations:

"And whatever ye shall ask in my name, that will I do, that the Father may be glorified in the Son." John 14:13 KJV

"If ye abide in me, and my words abide in you, ye shall ask what ye will, and it shall be done unto you." John 15:7

Daily Inspiration and Motivation:

We must, purpose in our hearts to execute the will of God for our lives.

The perfect will of God is what we must seek. The master always speaks. We must listen with our whole hearts. The permissive will of God sends us on detours.

Why not wait for Isaac, the promised child?

Seek to fulfill the will!

You're a Success Story....

Elevation prevails, and the prayer of the righteous avails.

We reached a summit of spiritual heights.

The fire lingers that the Holy Spirit ignites.

Beyond every moment of increasing glory is a great catharsis.... You're a success story.

2nd Corinthians 4:17 KJV "For our light affliction, which is but for a moment worketh for us or far more exceeding and eternal weight of glory."

The sun always shines again.

Your happiness is not orchestrated by man.

You are ready for your dreams to take flight.

You're going in, the right direction. You're God's delight.

Scriptural Affirmations:

"While we look not at the things which are seen, but at the things which are not seen: for the things which are seen are temporal; but the things which are not seen are eternal."

2nd Corinthians 4:18 KJV

Daily Affirmations and Motivation: Optimism is a great tool that promotes continued success. The drive is inside. "As a man thinketh in his heart, so is he." Believe in where God is taking you. Be ready to make your dream a reality. Manifestation starts with a dream. Action births the fruition of God's plains.

Born to Lead....

We are graced by the master to excel.

Even though we stumble, we ran well.

The crown is the ultimate incentive.

Premonitions are evident and preventive.

You are destined to progress and to succeed.

Though we may feel insignificant we were born to lead.

James 1:12 KJV "Blessed is the man that endureth temptation: For when he is tried, he shall receive the crown of life, which the Lord hath promised to them that love him."

Focus on the crown, not the cross.

The gains will supersede every loss.

Scriptural Affirmations:

23 "The steps of a good man are ordered by the Lord: and He delighteth in his way.

24 Though he fall, he shall not utterly be cast down: for the Lord upholdeth him with his hand."

Psalm 37:23-24 KJV

Daily Inspiration and Motivation:

Our ability to lead is innate. God bestowed upon us the necessary tools to attain the ultimate. We must keep our drive alive. The vital part of our success begins in the mind. "A man is a slave to whatever has mastered him."

With God leading, there will be much succeeding.

Don't get overwhelmed!
God is taking you to a greater realm.

A greater realm....

God is taking you to a higher realm of the spirit.

There's a new sound in the atmosphere designed for you to hear it.

Follow God's voice. It will enable you to decipher God's direction.

Yield, and submit to the divine hand of protection.

Never be discouraged or overwhelmed.

Know that God is taking you to a greater realm.

Psalm 42:7 KJV "Deep calleth unto deep at the noise of thy water sprouts: all thy waves and billows are gone over me."

Go where God is leading.

The angels are preceding.

Scriptural Affirmations:

"For therein is the righteousness of God revealed from faith to faith, as it is written, the just shall live by faith."

Romans 1:17 KJV

Daily Inspiration and Motivation: Don't focus on who left. Who stayed? That's enough to shout about. God will never leave you. That's quite reassuring. Regardless of who leaves, God will forever accompany you. Of course, we must always invite Him to stay. He's a gentleman. He always waits for the invitation to stay.

(Have a day filled with comfort and resolution for change.)

The Comforter has come...

Our times are quite perilous and perplexing indeed.

Where the cry for justice arises, there's an even greater need.

Tranquility evades us, and restitution seems bleak.

However, we're reminded of the promises God keeps.

There's a long road we've traveled from.

Solace has found some.

The comforter has come.

Isaiah 59:19 KJV "So shall they fear the name of the Lord from the west and His glory from the rising of the sun, when the enemy shall come in like a flood, the spirit of the Lord shall lift up a standard against him."

Scriptural Affirmations:

"But ye shall receive power, after that the Holy Ghost is come upon you: and ye shall be witnesses unto me both in Jerusalem, and in all Judaea, and in Samaria and unto the utmost part of the earth."

Acts 1:8 KJV

Daily Inspiration and Motivation: The Holy Spirit brings comfort and conviction. He's a guide. Once we accept Christ as Lord and Saviour of our lives, we can be filled with the Holy Spirit. There is mention of the Holy Spirit in the first and second chapters of the book of Acts. He arises after the crucifixion of Christ. He is here to seal the deal!

At the end of the tunnel....

Going through is painful indeed.

We fully appreciate times of plenty, when there are great needs.

We have to remain encouraged at all cost.

Focus on all the blessings we've gained instead of what we've lost.

It may have been illness, a hurricane, tornado, twister, a great flood, or stormy tunnel.

When you go through, you'll see the light at the end of the tunnel.

Romans 8:28 KJV "And we know all things work together for good to them that love God, to them who are called according to his purpose."

Count up the lost.

You gained more than you lost.

Scriptural Affirmations:

"What shall we then say to these things? If God be for us, who can be against us?"

Romans 8:31 KJV

"Nay, in all things we are more than conquerors through him that loved us."

Romans 8:37 KJV

Daily Inspiration and Motivation: No matter what we endure, there's always something good that arises from the experience. We can focus on the good that evolves. With every lesson, we acquire blessings. Focus on the good. Leave the bad in the past. Your anointing will be far greater because of "it!"

A new beginning...

Familiar scenes are far more picturesque when we view them with one who knows us best.

God will rule the setting obsolete when He delivers someone to make our lives complete.

All this time, you were inconceivably winning.

God was granting you a new beginning.

(The number 8 symbolizes new beginnings. Before the blessings began to manifest, I kept seeing the number 8 in many instances. God will give you signs to confirm His word. Watch for the signs.)

Isaiah 43:19 KJV Behold, I will do a new thing; it shall spring forth; shall ye not know it? I will even make a way in the wilderness [And] rivers in the desert.

God had to remove it.

He had to get you to it.

Scriptural Affirmations:

"And it shall come to pass in that day that his burden will be taken away from off thy shoulder, and his yoke from off thy neck, and the yoke shall be destroyed because of the anointing."

Isaiah 10:27 KJV

Daily Inspiration and Motivation:

God deals with us individually and collectively. Many assignments are the same. Some are different. God holds each of us accountable of fulfilling our assignments. We must obey God. Don't focus on the "some sayers", the "naysayers," or the "character assasinators". God is the judge of us all. He has the final say. It shall go His Way!

God turns our mourning into dancing. His word is forever enhancing.

Mourning into dancing...

When ability and agility are dissipating,

Innner strength transcends the damsel in waiting.

David's wife thought he was showing off no doubt.

However, it was the holy ghost inside him showing out.

Jesus is playing a love song. He's embracing and romancing.

It's not a performance. Jesus turned her mourning into dancing.

Isaiah 61:3 KJV "To appoint unto them that mourn in Zion, to give unto them beauty for ashes, joy for mourning, the garment of praise for the spirit of heaviness; that they might be called trees of righteousness, the planting of the Lord, that he might be glorified.

Your territory is about to expand. Just stand!

Scriptural Affirmations:

"Then David danced before the Lord with all his might; and David was wearing a linen ephod."

2nd Samuel 6:14 KJV

"And Miriam the prophetess, the sister of Aaron, took a timbrel in her hand and all the women went out after her with timbrels and with dances."

Exodus 15:20 KJV

Daily Inspiration and Motivation:

What God instilled within you is His gift to you. When you render your talents and gifts into service, it's your gift to God. When you give, God your all; He is not focused on your ability. He honors your availability. He's grooming you. You may be a diamond in the rough. Allow God to perform the metamorphosis and transformation. Watch the end product! It will blow your mind!

It was a Setup!

The setback was just a set up; so you could get up, stay up, wake up, stay prayed up, and keep your mind made up.

I will serve God until the day I die.

My goal is heaven! My limit is the sky!

Don't let the setback keep you back.

Arise! Snapback!

Let God attack!

Genesis 50:20 KJV But as for you, ye thought evil against me; but God meant it unto good, to bring to pass, as it is this day, to save much people alive.

Scriptural Affirmations:

"Many are the afflictions of the righteous: but the Lord delivereth him out of them all." Psalm 34:19 KJV

"If we suffer, we shall also reign with him: if we deny him, he also will deny us:"

2 Timothy 2:12 KJV

Daily Inspiration and Motivation:

The greatest achievements are birthed through the greatest adversity. God can take the worst mistakes and convert them into the most phenomenal messages. Our misery is our ministry, and it becomes our message. Let God use your story for His glory.

Everything is in the King....the Master

There's an ultimate dimension... a higher calling...

It brings a moment of Catharsis that one finds enthralling.

In this moment of awakenings, we find strength to shield and to envelope the uncertainties.

We rediscover what we once knew beyond reasonable doubt.

He's the shielder from adversity.

This voice inside me speaks when I find myself alone. It's hope in a disaster.

I found my everything! It's in the King.... the Master!

John 14:13 KJV "And whatsoever ye shall ask in my name, that will I do, that the Father maybe glorified in the Son."

You shall find His peace when you fervently seek.

Scriptural Affirmations:

"But the meek shall inherit the earth, and shall delight themselves in the abundance of peace." Psalm 37:11 KJV

"One thing have I desired of the Lord, that will I seek after, that I may dwell in the house of the Lord all the days of my life, to behold the beauty of the Lord, and to enquire in his temple." Psalm 27:4 KJV

Daily Inspiration and Motivation:

You derive at a place in God where nothing else matters. You realize that He validates, approves, and orchestrates. As long as He is pleased, you must go on. Some parts of this journey, you must travel alone. Internalize the lessons, and count all the blessings. God has it all under His control. Everyone won't accept what He instilled within you. Someone assigned to you needs to hear the reassurance. Someone is counting on you to stand. Your life is making a difference.

Speak to the Mountains!

Hindrances are mere stepping stones impeding the victory dance.

We are more than conquerors in every circumstance.

The opposition's making you. It won't be overtaking you.

Every essential need is met at the everlasting fountain.

Our faith ensures that we can speak to the mountains.

Mark 11:23 KJV "For verily I say unto you that whosoever shall say unto this mountain, Be thou removed; and be cast into the sea; and shall not doubt in his heart, but shall believe those things which he saith shall come to pass; he shall have whatsoever he saith."

Speak to the mountains!

You have access to everlasting fountains!

Scriptural Affirmations:

"If ye abide in me, and my words abide in you, ye shall ask what ye will, and it shall be done unto you." John 15:7 KJV

"Herein is my Father glorified that ye bear much fruit; so shall ye be my disciples."

John 15:8 KJV

Daily Inspiration and Motivation:

When oppositions arise, they are opportunities for God to show Himself strong. He performs His will in our lives. He just wants us to believe. We must be proactive in ushering the blessings in. God expects us to decree and to declare the blessings to be! When it's in God's will, we can have what we say!

You deserve joy unspeakable!

Joy is the precursor to strength unmeasured.

It's the happiness that one's hope has treasured.

Nothing compares to the love and joy of Christ, our King.

It instills within us the will to sing.

The melody lingers long after the stanzas end. It's reachable.

Stay happy. You deserve joy unspeakable.

Nehemiah 8:10 KJV

The joy of the Lord is your strength.

May all your goals be reachable.

May you have joy unspeakable.

Scriptural Affirmations:

"A merry heart doeth good like a medicine; but a broken spirit drieth the bones."

Proverbs 17:22 KJV

"Now unto Him that is able to do exceeding abundantly above all that we ask or think, according to the power that worketh in us," Ephesians 3:20 KJV

Daily Inspiration and Motivation:

Never let anyone or anything steal your joy. Remind the enemy about all God has already done on your behalf. God healed me from a brain tumor twice! He cancelled one brain surgery. The first time, the surgery was cancelled six days prior to the procedure. The neurosurgeon called me on the telephone, and he said, "Young lady, you are making a believer out of me. If I didn't know you had a brain tumor, I would have thought you never had one. I can't operate on a shadow." The second vision tests were the deciding factors for surgery. However, I had a 3ʳᵈ series of vision tests prior to the surgery date. All vision was within normal limits. Prior to this, I had begun to lose peripheral vision in both eyes. The word the ophthalmology team used was baffled. I'll share more in my next book/my testimonial manuscript. The second time, the brain tumor surgery was only discussed. After 2 consults, it was no longer discussed!

Soul Winning from the Beginning... All about souls...

In the midst of perilous and perplexing times, we need a personal relationship with Jesus Christ.

We must be sold out and committed. Be the living sacrifice.

All of us want to declare this race as won.

The ultimate victory is to hear the master say, "Well done!"

It's great to have endeavors and goals.

This walk with the Lord is all about souls.

Romans 10:9, 10 KJV

9 That if thou shalt confess with thy mouth the Lord Jesus, and shalt believe in thine heart that God raised Him from the dead, thou shalt be saved.

10 For with the heart man believeth unto righteousness; and with the mouth confession is made unto salvation.

This is the plan of salvation! Proclaim it unto the nations!

Scriptural Affirmations:

"If we confess our sins, he is faithful and just to forgive us our sins, and to cleanse us from all unrighteousness."

1st John 1:9 KJV

"And they said, Believe on the Lord Jesus Christ, and thou shalt be saved, and thy house."

Acts 16:31 KJV

Daily Inspiration and Motivation:

The plan of salvation is merely this, preaching Jesus and the crucifixion. If one believes that Jesus was crucified on the cross, and He arose again, he shall be saved. When someone wants to be saved, we can share Romans 10:9, 10. Explain that we must obey the commandments and live a consecrated and Holy life. Amen.

In Loving Memory..... (JG)
On behalf of her siblings

Farewell to our dear sister....

If love could have kept you here, you surely would have stayed.

The spirit of your zealous nature… The finesse shall forever be displayed.

You heard the voice of heaven calling. You saw the golden strewn paths and walls of emerald sparkling. How could you resist?

You danced right on into the heavens, though you knew you'd be tremendously missed.

You were the personification of an angel with such beauty heaven can heal.

We can't fully convey or even comprehend how much we miss her.

Rest on sweet angel. Farewell to our dear sister.

*We can hear your voice resonating, as you said, "I'm blessed and highly favored."

Your resounding phrase remains in our hearts, "I'm good, I'm good." You earned your crown as you persevered and labored!

Kaleidoscope...

The beauty of God's creations are quite picturesque.

They bring glory and joy causing one never to acquiesce.

The scenarios are far more beautiful than pictures have depicted.

When one fathoms what it beholds. He thinks not of being afflicted.

Even when uncertainty attempts to possess one's hope,

life's beauty overtakes one.

It's much like the array of a kaleidoscope!

Psalm 19:1 KJV "The heavens declare the glory of God; and the firmament showeth his handiwork."

It's is our duty to enjoy life's beauty.

Scriptural Affirmations:

"God makes everything beautiful in its time." Ecclesiastes 3:11 KJV

"God is a sun and a shield. The Lord will give grace, and glory: no good thing will He withhold from them that walk uprightly." Psalm 84:11 KJV

Daily Inspiration and Motivation:

I remember writing all my life. I would win awards for essays, poetry, and short stories. I wrote an essay in particular when I was in first grade. I won first place, and the prize was a kaleidoscope. I thought it was one of the most beautiful things I had ever seen. It was as though I had won a million dollars! I took my prize everywhere. It took me to lands unknown. I treasured it wholeheartedly. I would write more and more. Over my precious kaleidoscope, life was a lot like the vivid colors and abstract images. No matter what the combination, there was always a beauty found. Enjoy the colors of God's designs.

June 3, 2018   Age 51

Fabulously Fit...Blessed Fun at 51

I am intrigued and delighted in the passion ministry has ignited.

The fire of God catapults and compels me to attain my greater.

The King is my all. He's my infinite inspirator & motivator.

I'm never alone, for the Lord holds me close.

He sings me a love song.

In all things, and in every endeavor ... He lifts me to where I belong.

Now, ministry and medicine must coincide.

They are passions of mine that must collide.

Before the phenomenal day is done, I make a declaration.

I'm feeling fabulously fit & having blessed fun at 51!

Psalm 91:1,2 KJV

1 "He who dwelleth in the secret place of the most high shall abide under the shadow of the Almighty."

2 "He will say of the Lord, He is my refuge and my fortress, my God in Him will I trust."

I am unreservedly committed to the cause of Christ! I am nothing without the Lord! I love Him so!

Raging Waters...

Tumultuous turbulence precedes each crest.

Then comes the "calm!" It's the culmination of the test.

The catharsis reveals, "You maintained!"

Throughout the process, you were sustained.

Stamina has evolved for the unyielding sons and daughters.

We'll never succumb to the raging waters.

Psalm. 93:4 KJV "The Lord on high is mightier than the noise of many waters, yea, than the mighty waves of the sea."

As God's sons & daughters we can speak to the raging waters.

Scriptural Affirmations:

"The Lord reigneth; let the earth rejoice; let the multitude of isles be glad thereof."

Psalm 97:1 KJV

"…but the people that know their God shall be strong and do exploits." Daniel 11:32 KJV

Daily Inspiration and Motivation: The power is in the confession. We can speak "it" into existence. In God's will we can have what we say. We just have to activate our faith. Before we receive the miracle, God requires something from us. He generally gives specific instructions. Once we follow precisely, we receive the miracle, we must obey God at all cost.

The promise birthed perseverance

As a woman travails in the labor process,

Pain overwhelms her in this place of distress.

In the final push, the "crowning" emerges.

The child is her treasure. Like a miracle, she births it.

Nearly overcome by pain, the mother resonates, "It was all worth it."

There was much tenacity and adherence.

The process and the promise birthed perseverance.

Psalm 113:9 KJV "He maketh the barren woman to keep house, and to be a joyful mother of children. Praise ye the Lord."

The birthing was spiritual and transforming.

Yes, it was quite painful, but heartwarming.

Scriptural Affirmations:

"For I know the thoughts that I think toward you, saith the Lord, thoughts of peace, and not of evil, to give you an expected end." Jeremiah 29:11 KJV

"Delight thyself also in the Lord: and He shall give thee the desires of thine heart."

Psalm 37:4 KJV

Daily inspiration and Motivation:

Anything worth having is worth pursuing. When we are about to give birth to something greater, the labor pains become quite intense. If we can endure the contractions, we'll give birth to the blessing. Press! Push! Persevere! Praise! Pray!

God is the author of our story.
He can make our life a Best Seller!

Author of your story...

Your greatest testimony has not been recorded.

All your efforts shall be rewarded.

God wasn't considering your qualifications.

He called you to the nations.

There will be miracles, peace, and glory.

Allow God to be the author of your story.

Hebrews 12:2 KJV "Looking unto Jesus the author and finisher of our faith; who for the joy that was set before Him endured the cross, despising shame, and is set down at the right hand of the throne of God."

Even the misunderstanding and shame will bring glory.

Just allow God to be the author of your story.

Scriptural Affirmations:

"For our light, affliction, which is but for a moment, worketh for us a far more exceeding and eternal weight of glory;"

"While we look not at the things which are seen, but at the things which are not seen: for the things which are seen are temporal; but the things which are not seen are eternal."

2nd Corinthians 4:17, 18 KJV

Daily Inspiration and Motivation: No one knows us the way God does. God is the best selling Author of all time. As we yield to Him, He takes control of the pen. He creates a masterpiece of our life story. It always brings Him glory. There's good and bad, victories and defeat. God renders our story complete. It is a best seller!

In Love with The Lord...

In the midnight hour, he holds us tenderly in an embrace.

Shielded from the darkest days, our sorrows are erased.

We reminisce of many times of happiness and bliss.

He holds us ever so gently.

Every moment is sealed with a kiss.

Even in times of uncertainty, things never seem too hard.

There's such ecstasy in this encounter. I'm so in love with the Lord.

1st Corinthians 13:7 KJV

"Beareth all things, believeth all things, hopeth all things, endureth all things."

His love is infinite and simply divine.

Nothing compares with God's love. It's oh so fine!

Scriptural Affirmations:

"But God commendeth his love toward us, in that, while we were yet sinners, Christ died for us." Romans 5:8 KJV

"Greater love hath no man than this, that a man lay down His life for his friends." John 15:13 KJV

Daily Inspiration and Motivation:

God's love for us is unconditional

Even when we stumble, He's there to lovingly bring restoration! There's just no other comfort comparable! It's a sweet perfume that anoints the atmosphere! It's a consuming fire that burns within. We can keep on loving on the Lord! In Him nothing is deemed insurmountable or too hard! Greater things are on the horizon indeed! It all started with a seed.

Mover of Mountains...

The omnipotent one curved every masterpiece.... creator of the heavens and earth!

He went on to shape and form all that was. It gave way to the universe.

The mountain's valley and peaks, the King formed them all.

Every stream, river, hill, the sun the stars... He spoke, and there were pristine waterfalls.

The giver of gifts, summoned forth life changing fountains.

He was all! He is all!

We worship the King! The declaration evolved. He's the mover of mountains!

Matthew 17:20 KJV "If ye have faith as the grain of a mustard seed, ye shall say unto this mountain, remove hence to yonder place and it shall remove, and nothing shall be impossible unto you."

* Speak to the land and the sea!

In the will, nothing shall be impossible unto thee!

Scriptural Affirmations:

"So then faith cometh by hearing, and hearing by the word of God." Romans 10:17

"But without faith, it is impossible to please him: for he that cometh to god must believe that he is, and that he is a rewarder of them that diligently seek him." Hebrews 11:6

Daily Inspiration and Motivation: We can stand on the word of God in every facet of our lives. Nothing supersedes God's awesomeness. He's just bad all by Himself. When we see and partake in all His wondrous creations, it's mystifying! Nothing's more majestic or pristine! Everything the human intellect attempts to fathom His infinity, God performs another miracles. The seed of His greatness breathed life resurrected all that was dormant and dissonant! The King proclaimed it to be. It's transforming! Honor the King of Kings in all His amazing things. It's a joy to serve Him.

Trust God's Plan!

Complacency is never the place God intends.

Some instances He breaks and other times, He bends! His timing is impeccable!

He always knows best.

Let Him guide you during the test.

Oftentimes, the answers evade us! We don't fully understand.

God grants peace of mind. Trust God's plan.

Romans 8:28 KJV "And we know that all things work together for good, to them that love God, to them are called according to His purpose."

You're right on point.

God favors, blesses, appoints, and anoints.

Scriptural Affirmations:

"Nay in all things, we are are more than conquerors through him that loved us." Romans 8:37 KJV

"The blessings of the Lord, it maketh rich, and he addeth no sorrow with it." Proverbs 10:22 KJV

Daily Inspiration and Motivation: You can stand on every affirmation in the word of God! He speaks so profoundly to our spirit man. We are never left without instructions. Your faith has touched God! He will honor your obedience and your unyielding faith. In the will you shall have what you say, decree and declare it. Watch God more. He will do "the hard thing"! Only believe!

This is a special entry:

Your continued support is much appreciated, Glory to God for broadcast, "Activate your Faith!" It airs on Monday through Friday at 4:30pm Central time on Preach the Word Worldwide Network Television.

Activate your Faith...

It's all in what you've heard in God's compelling and life changing word.

There's a leap from deep within.

We grasp a word that coerces us to win.

The drive enables us to move out of complacency! We no longer wait!

That's our "denouement" moment when we "Activate our Faith!"

Romans 10:17 KJV "So then faith cometh by hearing, and hearing, by the word of God."

You can step out on all God's word you've processed and heard.

"Scriptural Affirmations:

But when Jesus heard it, he answered him saying, Fear not: believe only, and she shall be made whole." Luke 8:50 KJV

"When Jesus heard it, he marveled, and said to them that followed, Verily I say unto you, I have not found so great faith, no, not in Israel." Matthew 8:10 KJV

Daily Inspiration and Motivation:

You have mountain moving faith inside you. God is backing you. You and God have this.

Keep on marching towards destiny. God has accompanied you all your life. He would never forsake or leave you now. No, no one has reached perfection. All of us have made mistakes. No, we don't have all the answers, but we have God. He has all the answers. He is omniscient, omnipotent, and omnipresent. What a mighty God we serve. Take a leap of faith. Only believe! In the will, the prophecies shall be fulfilled.

God's heavenly creations bring blessed sensations!

Majestic Splendor...

It's even more beautiful than pictures depict it to be.

There's far more embedded than what we see.

From the picturesque waterfalls of Hawaii and the magnificence of "La Tour Eiffel" in Paris, France! There's an eternal "beat" to the music that causes our feet to dance.

To all hearts once torn, God is the mender.

Oh what a joy to behold the majestic splendor.

Ecclesiastes 3:11 KJV "He hath made all things beautiful in His time..."

Enjoy the heavenly creations across the nations.

Scriptural Affirmations:

"In the beginning, God created the heavens and the earth." Genesis 1:1 KJV

"The earth is the Lord's and the fulness thereof; the world, and they that dwell therein." Psalm 24:1 KJV

Daily Inspiration and Motivation:

Just as God placed beauty in everything He touched, that same beauty is in you. God graced you with a uniqueness and creativity. Utilize each and every gift He put inside you. There's greatness upon and inside you! Shine everyday of your life. One day, God will summon each of us back to Him. We have to be prepared to meet Him.

Burden bearer...
(We can rest in the Lord.)

The answers escape us! We realize it wasn't a dream. We're awake.

God knows the depth of all sorrows. Unequivocally, He never makes mistakes.

Give it all to Him. He's got your heart in His hands.

All things must hearken to His commands.

He'll wipe away all tears!

Trust the heavy load sharer.

What a joy He conveys! He's the burden bearer.

Matthew 11:28 KJV "Come unto me all ye that labor, and are heavy laden, I will give you rest."

We all need the King of Kings in all things.

Scriptural Affirmations:

"Take my yoke upon you, and learn of me; for I am meek and lowly in heart: and ye shall find rest unto your souls." Matthew 11:29 KJV

"God is our refuge and our strength, a very present help in trouble." Psalm 46:1 KJV

Daily Inspiration and Motivation:

When we are weak, we are made strong. His word is filled with encouragement, unspeakable joy, love, comfort, and peace. While the nations are praying, God is working behind the scenes. God calleth those things that be not as though they were. Hearts are heavy but God is bearing the burdens. Rest in Him. He's got everything in His hands.

Power in Prayer....

Prayer makes the difference in everything we face!

All the burdens are lifted! They're annihilated without a trace.

When we so fervently seek Him, we will always reach Him.

Before we're on the scene, God is already there.

We can always petition the Lord.

There's great power in prayer.

James 5:16 KJV "Confess your faults, one to another, and pray one for another, that ye may be healed. The effectual fervent prayer of a righteous man availeth much."

Give it to God in prayer. He is forever there!

Scriptural Affirmations:

"And he spake a parable unto them to this end, that men ought always to pray, and not faint;" Luke 18:1 KJV

"Pray without ceasing." 1st Thessalonians 5:17 KJV

Be careful for nothing; but in every thing by prayer and supplication with thanksgiving let your requests be made known unto God. Philippians 4:6 KJV

Daily Inspiration and Motivation: God can figure it out all the time. When we can't fathom the antidote, God has it all worked out. We can rest assured that God will answer. He's got it all secured! All the cares can be released to Him. When we do our part, the master will forever perform on our behalf. There's no cause to be overwhelmed. We are more than conquerors!

Tribute to Kobe & Gianna Bryant

I express sincere condolences and prayers to the Bryant family and all the families who lost loved ones in the untimely incident. You'll meet again.

Mansion in the sky...

Words evade me as I ponder their escape to the distant shore.

They fly with wings. On this side, we'll see them no more. However, it's not good-bye.

It's just farewell.

The legacy of greatness remains here for us to tell.

Daddy and daughter are sharing an eternal dance in the sky.

Now, they run amid the courts in heaven. They fly high.

We're deeply saddened, but daddy and daughter share a beautiful mansion in the sky.

1st Corinthians 15:54 KJV "So when this corruptible shall have put on incorruption, and this mortal shall have put on immortality, then shall be brought to pass the saying that is written, death is swallowed up in victory."

Death shall one day be no more.

We'll walk hand in hand on heaven's shore.

Scriptural Affirmations:

"Wherefore comfort one another with these words." 1st Thessalonians 4:18 KJV

"O Death, where is thy sting? O grave, where is thy victory?" 1st Corinthians 15:55 KJV

Daily Inspiration and Motivation:

Death shall be no more. God's word assures us that weeping may endure for a night, but joy cometh in the morning. We never know when God will call us home. We can live a life that prepares us for heaven. My heart goes out to the Bryant family and all the other families affected. May God strengthen and comfort them all. May they have peace. When all is said and done, our focus to make it to heaven. No one nor anything can impede or stop what God has prepared for you. God is your source.

Jehovah Jireh...

God has never forsaken his own.

All your life, He's provided! You've grown.

Satan knows he can't defeat a child of God. You always arise.

Stay focused! Keep your eyes on the prize.

When you reminisce, hasn't God always provided?

You can forever rely on Jehovah Jireh.

Psalm 24:1 KJV "The earth is the Lord's and the fullness thereof, the world and they that dwell therein."

Stay with God from beginning to the end.

Trust His plan! Jehovah Jireh always wins.

Scriptural Affirmations:

"But my God shall supply all your need according to His riches in glory by Jesus Christ." Philippians 4:19 KJV

"Give, and it shall be given unto you; good measure, pressed down, and shaken together, and running over, shall men give into your bosom. For with the same measure that ye mete withal it shall be measured to you again."

Luke 6:38 KJV

Daily Inspiration and Motivation:

When the enemy realizes that God has been providing for us all our life he is going to flee. Rest in the will of God, His God's timing is always perfect. It doesn't matter who thinks you shouldn't have it! God said, "It's yours!" Go get it!

God's favor reigns!
The losses never supersede the gains!

Favor surrounds you and me!

Putting our trust in the master is never misappropriated.

We can rely on His plan. In Him we're move than validated.

When we talk to Him, He performs.

In the world, we must never conform.

In Christ, there's always victory.

Keep pressing for the favor surrounds you and me.

Proverbs 3:4 KJV "So shalt thou find favor and good understanding in the sight of God and man."

All shall favor you and I.

We're destined for a greater prize.

Scriptural Affirmations:

"But let patience have her perfect work that ye may be perfect and entire, wanting nothing." James 1:4 KJV

"Keep thy heart with all diligence; for out of it are the issues of life." Proverbs 4:23 KJV

Daily Inspiration and Motivation: Be watchful in all things. God has been with you since the beginning. He shall always be here for you. Continue in your kingdom assignments. God has sent His angels innumerable times. He will strengthen that which remains. God has it. God has you. Do not give the enemy any ammunition to work with. God is securing the bay. Keep Him in every decision.

God is still opening doors! The next one's yours!

Keep Seeking...

The universe is a canvas of new opportunities and vision.

We'll excel including God in every decision.

Venturing out into uncertainty brings new hope and diversity.

God will never stops speaking.

We just have to forever keep seeking.

Matthew 7:7 KJV "Ask, and it shall be given you; Seek, and ye shall find; Knock, and it shall be opened unto you."

Seek Him to reach Him.

Scriptural Affirmations:

"As the deer panteth after the water brooks, so panteth my soul after thee, O God." Psalm 42:1 KJV

"Delight thyself also in the Lord: and he shall give thee the desires of thine heart.

Psalm 37:4 KJV

Daily Inspiration and Motivation:

As long as you remain connected to the power source, you are in the best hands! God will light your way. He will open doors no one can close. You can't lose focus, especially now. This is the season when God well perform "the deemed to be insurmountable" thing. It's absolutely mind blowing! God will light your way! Watch what He's about to do on your behalf! Some things He will do just so He doesn't look bad! He put His name on the line just for you! He's bad all by Himself! You are carrying His spiritual DNA! You are a blueprint of Him! Somebody ought to go on ahead, and give God some praise right here! I went on in on this one!

It all comes down to two words, "Well done!"

"Well Done!"

When God is for you, you have eagle's wings

You soar, and you conquer the greatest of things.

No weapon formed against you shall prosper.

Keep living what you preach.

God is exemplified in your walk, your smile, and in the prophetic words you speak.

Continue to be a light!

Darkness shall never prevail.

Everything God touches, it fruitfully avails.

At the day's end, a soul's heart mends. Salvation comes, and the battle is won.

God smiles upon your life, lovingly says, "Well Done!"

Matthew 25:23 KJV "His Lord said unto Him, Well done, good and faithful servant; thou hast been faithful over a few things, I will make thee ruler over many things: Enter thou unto the joy of the Lord."

Once the race is won, God will say, "Well done!"

Scriptural Affirmations:

"Confess your faults one to another, and pray one for another, that ye may be healed. The effectual fervent prayer of a righteous man availeth much." James 5:16 KJV

"For me wrestle not against flesh and blood, but against principalities, against powers, against the rulers the of the darkness of this world, against spiritual wickedness in high places." Ephesians 6:12 KJV

Daily Inspiration and Motivation:

If they are fellowshipping with your enemies, cut them off. God will expose your enemies. He already showed you their fate. "For the wages of sin is death; but the gift of God is eternal life through Jesus Christ our Lord." Romans 6:23 When the wrath of God falls, no one wants to be in the line of fire. Peter can be restored, but you have to dismiss Judas. Tell Judas, good-bye. Be vigilant. Watch the occult be uncovered and exposed. "This" elevated you to a greater realm of the spirit. Your discernment shall be keener. (Selah)

All things are made new!
New opportunities, new mindset,
new jobs, new positions, new blessings,
fresh and new anointings...

On the move...

Relinquish the old when God directs.

God's bestowing upon you the new.

A new mindset is birthed when joy is what you pursue.

Anticipation births manifestation of God's finest things.

When you remain focused, there's such a peace it brings.

When it's tranquility and solace you possess, you can't lose.

Beloved, remain the course you're already on the move!

Habakkuk 2:3 KJV "For the vision is yet for an appointed time, but at the end it shall speak, and not lie: though it tarry, wait for it; because it will surely come, it will not tarry."

God's already giving you the new.

Just wait and see where He takes you to.

Scriptural Affirmations:

"But as it is written, Eye hath not seen, nor ear heard, neither have entered into the heart of man, the things which God hath prepared for those that love Him."

1st Corinthians 2:9 KJV

"For I know the thoughts that I think toward you, saith the Lord, are thoughts of peace, and not of evil, to give you an expected end." Jeremiah 29:11 KJV

Daily Inspiration and Motivation: Keep excelling. God is already honoring His promises for 2020. The greatest adversities birth the greatest miracles. I've had plenty in 2020. We shall overcome the hardships. Every struggle has an expiration date. All I can say is, "Thank you Jesus!" This too shall pass!

Prayers to heal societal ills:

Praying for the nations:

Heavenly Father bestow upon us a sweet release of world peace.

Gracious God, touch the minds, and touch the people's hearts.

May we lean today on your holy word and all that it imparts.

As your sons and daughters, and voices of future generations,

We give you all the glory and honor. We are praying for the nations.

Philippians 4:7 "And the peace of God, which passeth all understanding, shall keep your hearts and minds through Jesus Christ."

God brings peace to the world's nations.

May we preserve the future generations.

Scriptural Affirmations:

"And this gospel of the kingdom shall be preached in all the world for a witness unto all nations; and then the end shall come". Matthew 24:14 KJV

"And he said unto them, Go ye into all the world, and preach the gospel to every creature." Mark 16:15 KJV

Daily Inspiration and Motivation:

There's a mandate on our lives. Regardless, we have to preach the gospel to all the nations of the world.

We must stand along with the masses of Christians all over the hemispheres to proclaim the gospel of the kingdom. May we always have a heart to proclaim salvation!

Preachers reaching the nations....

Beautiful Feet...

They journey to lands afar and near.

God prepared their way. He alleviated their fear.

They walk worthy of the vocation.

They serve future generations.

Souls are birthed throughout the world's nations.

They embrace all! Strangers they never meet.

They carry the gospel! They have beautiful feet.

Isaiah 52:7 KJV "How beautiful upon the mountains are the feet of Him that bringeth good tidings, that publisheth peace; that bringeth good tidings of good things, that publisheth salvation; that sayeth unto Zion, thy God reigneth.

They have a style of their own.

Beautiful feet bear the miles they've gone.

Scriptural Affirmations:

"But watch in all things, endure afflictions, do the work of an evangelist, make full proof of thy ministry." 2nd Timothy 4:5 KJV

"Wherefore take unto you the whole armour of God, that ye may be able to withstand in the evil day, and having done all, to stand." Ephesians 6:13 KJV

Daily Inspiration and Motivation: The words speak of those who carry the gospel. They have "beautiful feet." The applicable message is that they travel to lands, far and near. God orchestrates and guides them wherever they go! They travel! They're on the move to bless the world with the word of God. I join the ranks of those who preach the gospel to the nations. The encounters, appearances, demeanors, and experiences are somewhat diverse. However, the goal is the same. All are soul winners for Christ. Keep reaching the world with the word of God.

Divine Deliverance International Outreach Ministries celebrated one year of ministry in September 2019. We have a lifetime to go. To God be all the Glory!

First year...

God gave us miracles of financial breakthroughs, blessings, and healings.

He gave us two worldwide television broadcasts in year one. He's forever sealing.

Everything God seals is truly well done.

We have a long journey ahead, but we celebrate from whence we've come.

Look how for God has brought us from.

These are times we treasure and hold dear.

God brought us triumphantly throughout the first year.

Philippians 1:6 KJV "Being confident of this very thing, that he which hath begun a good work in you will perform it until the day of Jesus Christ."

This is only the beginning.

In Christ, we're winning.

Scriptural Affirmations:

"For we are His workmanship, created in Christ Jesus unto good works, which God hath before ordained that we should walk in them." Ephesians 2:10 KJV

"And He said unto them go ye into all the world, and preach the gospel to every creature." Mark 16:15 KJV

Daily Inspiration and Motivation: We all have kingdom assignments. Some are different. Many are the same. However, the goal is still souls! We can defeat the kingdom of dark by continuing to proclaim the gospel in whatever platform God has blessed us with. I declared my ministry as international before its inception. Look what the Lord has done! He gave us worldwide television platforms. God gave us tremendous favor with great CEOs and owners of television networks. We don't take it lightly. I love you Preach the World Worldwide Network Television. Much life! Much Love! Muah!

Favor surrounds you and me...

Putting our trust in the Master is never misappropriated.

We can rely on His plan! In him, we're more than validated!

When we talk to Him, He performs!

In the world, we must never conform.

In Christ, there's always victory!

Keep pressing for the promises! Favor surrounds you and me.

Proverbs 3:4 KJV "So shalt thou find favor and good understanding in the sight of God and man."

All shall favor you and me!

We're destined for greater you see!

Scriptural Affirmations:

"But let patience have her perfect work, that ye may be perfect and entire, wanting nothing." James 1:4 KJV

"Keep thy heart with all diligence; for out of it are the issues of life." Proverbs 4:23 KJV

Daily Inspiration and Motivation:

God has been with you since the beginning, and He shall be with you until He bids you to come. Live for Him. Complete your kingdom assignments. God has provided for you, and He sent His angels. He will give strength to those remaining. God has "IT!" God had you! Don't give the enemy any ammunition to work with! God is securing the bag. Keep Him in every decision!

The smile speaks...

Through it all, I smile!

It was worth it all… every test, every trial!

Our smile leads the way!

It illuminates the darkest day!

Worship and praise erupts! Joy evolves!

Every dilemma or problem we present to the master, He solves!

God is for you! That's enough to know God's for keeps!

Come what may, You have unspeakable joy! The smile speaks!

Nehemiah 8:10 KJV "…for the joy of the Lord is your strength."

A thousand words are in a picture indeed!

It starts with a smile. God cultivates the seed!

Scriptural Affirmations:

"Now unto Him that is able to do exceeding abundantly above all that we ask or think, according to the power that worketh in us," Ephesians 3:20 KJV

"But as it is written, Eye hath not seen, nor ear heard, neither have entered in the heart of man, the things which God has prepared for them that love Him."

1st Corinthians 2:9 KJV

Daily Inspiration and Motivation:

When you see the smile, you realize all the joy! Just having God to love, to protect, and to watch over us all brings overwhelming joy! God loves us so! That's enough to bring a neverending smile! It's so awesome to hear people tell me that I am always smiling! They say it blesses them, and it makes them smile! (On my jobs, travels, everywhere I go…) I'm so happy that I made it! I'm still here! I give God everything I have left inside!

Road to Success...

What God has given you is unique,

And it deems you complete!

God knows your heart, and He sees the fruit everyday.

Keep living by the word. Live by what God continues to convey.

What God requires is our best!

You can expect Him to do the rest!

Stay on the road to success!

1st Samuel 16:7 KJV "…man looks at the outward appearance, but God looketh at the heart."

Cleave to what God says is right.

Love Him with your whole heart!

Remain in the fight!

Scriptural Affirmations:

"For I know the thoughts that I think toward you, saith the Lord, thoughts of peace, and not of evil, to give you an expected end." Jeremiah 29:11 KJV

"Being confident of this very thing, that He which hath begun a good work in you will perform it until the day of Jesus Christ:" Philippians 1:6 KJV

Daily Inspiration and Motivation:

The honorable Bishop T. D. Jakes summed it up best! He said he preached to two people in the back woods of Virginia as though He was preaching to thousands. Now, God has given him thousands to preach to. The applicable message is, "Never disdain the beginning of something great!" God is going to continue to blow your mind! Live in expectancy of even greater miracles, blessings, promotions, elevations, ministries, jobs, positions, and accomplishments!

Your gifts uplift!

God honors availability! He's there during every test!

He "views" every effort! Just give Him your very best!

The Bible says to "stir up the gifts!"

Souls are birthed!

The kingdom needs you throughout the nations of the earth!

Whether strong, gentle, graceful, or swift…

The kingdom can utilize all! Your gifts uplift!

2nd Timothy 1:6 KJV "Wherefore I put thee in remembrance that thou stir up the gift of God, which is in thee by the putting on of hands."

Sing unto the Lord! Dance! Leap!

God needs you! It's all for keeps!

Scriptural Affirmations:

"Sing unto Him, sing psalms unto Him: talk ye of His wondrous works." Psalm 105:2

"And David danced before the Lord with all his might; and David was girded with a linen ephod." 2nd Samuel 6:14 KJV

Daily Inspiration and Motivation:

All of us have gifts and talents that are vital to the kingdom. Everyone has an opinion, but God has dominion! God is backing you up! The servant who had five talents, utilized his, and he received five more. The one who had two talents utilized his, and he gained two more. Jesus said, "Well done thy good and faithful servant. Thou hast been faithful over a few things, come on higher, and I'll make thee ruler over many things." The servant who had one talent, buried his in the sand. God gave his to the one that had ten talents. The moral of the story is, "If we don't use it, we'll lose it!"

Blessings Galore...

Many avenues for revenue God has revealed!

All His promises are on the scene...

signed and sealed!

We must express our gratitude in all things always!

I've had a horn of plenty in 2020...in all my days!

We'll see innumerable blessings... more than ever before!

Children of the most high God! Be in expectancy of "blessings galore!"

"Every good and perfect gift is from above, and cometh down from the Father of lights, with whom is no variableness, neither shadow of turning."

James 1:17 KJV

Blessings come in innumerable ways!

Give God thanks and glory all of your days!

Scriptural Affirmations:

"Bless the Lord, O my soul: and all that is within me, bless His holy name." Psalm 103:1 KJV

"In everything give thanks: for this is the will of God in Christ Jesus concerning you."

1st Thessalonians 5:18 KJV

Daily Inspiration and Motivation:

I'm so grateful to God for being who He is! If people only knew your story... I have great testimonies birthed through adversity and challenges! I must say that God always comes through! Messages were birthed through miracles! The greater the battles, the greater the rewards! "It is good for me that I have been afflicted; that I might learn thy statutes." Psalm 119:71 The battles are a setup for all your triumphs to come into fruition! You stand no matter what comes! I'm standing in the gap on your behalf! I pray, and I fast on our behalf! God loves you, and I do too!

Forever grateful to the King!

"Sovereign" depicts His awesomeness as He so triumphantly reigns!

No one supersedes His "excellency" as the Holy word explains!

We could never express enough "Thanks" or mere adoration!

He's the "great" I am! What an instant "gratification!"

I'm captivated how He makes the soul and the heart sing!

Oh my, how I'm forever grateful to the King!

Psalm 24:8 KJV "Who is the King of glory? The Lord strong and mighty, the Lord mighty in battle."

Keep on loving on the King!

Reverence Him more than anything!

Scriptural Affirmations:

"Lift up your heads, O ye gates; and be ye lift up ye everlasting doors; and the King of glory shall come in." Psalm 24:7 KJV

"Who is the King of glory? The Lord strong and mighty, the Lord mighty in battle." Psalm 24:8 KJV

Daily Inspiration and Motivation:

In all of His majestic splendor, He still finds the time to attend to our needs! He watches over His word to perform it in our lives! Who wouldn't love and adore Him? He's just so marvelous being who He is to all of us! What an exceedingly great joy to worship and to serve Him! He is my everything! He's Christ, my King! God made you Amazing!

...Forever rejoice!

Your smile causes the heart to dance! It's a gift!

In many instances, it comforts and lifts!

Infinity and all things originate from "the King!"

We can acknowledge Him in each and everything!

Know that happiness, peace, and solace bring such joy! It's the ultimate choice!

Everyday and in all things, "Forever rejoice!"

Philippians 4:4 KJV "Rejoice in the Lord always, and again I say rejoice."

Your smile is a light!

Let it guide you "through" the fight!

Scriptural Affirmations:

16 "Rejoice forevermore."

17 "Pray without ceasing."

1st Thessalonians 5:16,17 KJV

"A merry heart doeth good like a medicine: but a broken spirit drieth the bones." Proverbs 17:22 KJV

Daily Inspiration and Motivation:

Follow after still waters and quiet streams. "Good success" is always on the other side of happiness. When you follow God's divine instructions, you can always expect heavenly productions. Capitalize on the "SELAH" moments. Progress is always best. There's a force attempting to orchestrate your downfall or demise! God's plan is for you to succeed, and He forever meets all the needs! He's the BEST friend you could ever have! Lean on Him!

Good success...

It's when the drive to excel summons and compels!

Your gaze is fixed upon the promises! You run well!

This is the exceeding great joy that the Bible portrays.

Live in the prosperity of God's plan all of your days!

When you know you're giving God your best, It's the ultimate test!

You've embarked upon your journey to "Good Success!"

Joshua 1:8 KJV "This book of the law shall not depart out of thy mouth but thou shalt meditate therein day and night, that thou mayest observe to do accordingly to all that is written therein: Then shalt thou make thy way prosperous, and then thou shalt have good success."

Look beyond the test!

Only see victory and "Good Success!"

Scriptural Affirmations:

"They that sow in tears, shall reap in joy."

Psalm 126:5 KJV

Thou hast turned my mourning into dancing: thou hast put off my sackcloth, and girded me with gladness." Psalm 30:11 KJV

Daily Inspiration and motivation:

God is reminding us of His faithfulness. If we just think to mention it to Him, He performs it in His will! His miracles, signs, and wonders continuously follow those who dare to believe! God is making you living PROOF of His POWER! LIVE! LAUGH! LOVE! THE BLOOD OF JESUS COVERS IT ALL! MUCH LIFE! MUCH LOVE! MUAH! (KISSES TO ALL!)

Printed in the United States
By Bookmasters